D0765192

GENE
EVERLASTING

OTHER BOOKS BY GENE LOGSDON

Fiction:

Pope Mary and the Church of Almighty Good Food
The Last of the Husbandmen
The Lords of Folly

Nonfiction:

A Sanctuary of Trees
Holy Shit
Small-Scale Grain Raising
The Contrary Farmer's Invitation to Gardening
The Pond Lovers
The Mother of All Arts
All Flesh Is Grass
You Can Go Home Again
Good Spirits: A New Look at Ol' Demon Alcohol
Living at Nature's Pace
The Contrary Farmer
The Low-Maintenance House
Gene Logsdon's Practical Skills
Organic Orcharding: A Grove of Trees to Live in
Two-Acre Eden
Getting Food from Water: A Guide to Backyard Aquaculture
The Gardener's Guide to Better Soil
Successful Berry Growing
Homesteading: How to Find New Independence on the Land
*Wyeth People: A Portrait of Andrew Wyeth as Seen
by His Friends and Neighbors*

GENE EVERLASTING

$\mathcal{A}$ CONTRARY FARMER'S THOUGHTS
$\mathcal{ON}$ LIVING FOREVER

GENE LOGSDON

Chelsea Green Publishing
White River Junction, Vermont

The cover illustrations and the illustrations on pages 1, 9, 17, 25, 35, 41, 45, 51, 57, 67, 77, 85, 99, 107, 115, 123, 137, 143, and 155 are reproduced from the Educational Technology Clearinghouse ClipArt ETC collection with permission of the Florida Center for Instructional Technology (http://etc.usf.edu/clipart).

The illustration on page 21 is from Wikimedia Commons (http://commons.wikimedia.org/wiki /File:Killdeer_(PSF).png).

Project Manager: Bill Bokermann
Project Editor: Benjamin Watson
Copy Editor: Laura Jorstad
Proofreader: Helen Walden
Designer: Melissa Jacobson

Printed in the United States of America.
First printing January, 2014.
10 9 8 7 6 5 4 3 2 1   14 15 16 17 18

Our Commitment to Green Publishing

Chelsea Green sees publishing as a tool for cultural change and ecological stewardship. We strive to align our book manufacturing practices with our editorial mission and to reduce the impact of our business enterprise in the environment. We print our books and catalogs on chlorine-free recycled paper, using vegetable-based inks whenever possible. This book may cost slightly more because it was printed on paper that contains recycled fiber, and we hope you'll agree that it's worth it. Chelsea Green is a member of the Green Press Initiative (www.greenpressinitiative.org), a nonprofit coalition of publishers, manufacturers, and authors working to protect the world's endangered forests and conserve natural resources. *Gene Everlasting* was printed on FSC®-certified paper supplied by Maple Press that contains at least 30% postconsumer recycled fiber.

Library of Congress Cataloging-in-Publication Data
Logsdon, Gene.
  Gene everlasting : a contrary farmer's thoughts on living forever / Gene Logsdon.
      pages cm
  ISBN 978-1-60358-539-2 (hardcover) — ISBN 978-1-60358-540-8 (ebook)
1. Logsdon, Gene. 2. Cancer—Patients—Psychology. 3. Death—Psychological aspects. 4.
Longevity—Psychological aspects. I. Title. II. Title: Contrary farmer's thoughts on living forever.
  RC265.6.L64A3 2014
  362.19699'40092—dc23
  [B]

                                        2013040398

Chelsea Green Publishing
85 North Main Street, Suite 120
White River Junction, VT 05001
(802) 295-6300
www.chelseagreen.com

MIX
Paper from
responsible sources
FSC® C068106
www.fsc.org

Contents

PREFACE

❖

*A*fter I became a cancer survivor, I started to think more about the meaning of mortality and immortality, naturally enough. As I did so, I noticed that a whole lot of other people were doing the same, even though most of them were perfectly healthy. It occurred to me that the more humans disconnected themselves from nature, the more fearful they became of the most natural event in life, that is, death. Maybe that was just my imagination since death has always been feared, but everywhere there seemed to be more novel and imaginative examples of death dread. The priesthood of the Internet was offering a service that would give us the ability to tweet online forever. "When your heart stops beating, you'll keep on tweeting," said the advance publicity for electronic immortality.

At about the same time, Venezuela's president Hugo Chávez died and his body was being "embalmed for posterity" as in the days of the pharaohs. Although it didn't really end up that way, his remains would have been "preserved" and displayed in a museum "forever." This struck me as more pathetic than tweeting after death or even freezing dying bodies in the hope that future science could thaw the cadavers out and overhaul them for another run at tweeting in real time. But mummification, however defined, was hardly any more pitiable as a pathway to immortality than the many religious and secular efforts to find life everlasting up there in the misty regions of space everlasting. My computer repairman told me I no longer needed to worry about losing any of my precious words in my document files because they were being automatically backed up in "the Cloud," where they would remain inviolate as long as the Electron God so ordained.

Then I learned, as if current events were bent on helping me talk my publisher into doing this book, that so-called death cafés were becoming popular. The first one, as far as I could research, took place in England in 2011, and by 2012 they were all over. Death cafés are gatherings of people who want to talk about dying while dining on tea and cake, or hopefully over alcoholic spirits (the only kind of spirits I am sure exists). The popularity of something seemingly so macabre appeared to stem from an increasing unwillingness to accept religious teachings about life after death. Parental thoughts about going to heaven and spending eternity happily in the arms of Jesus didn't satisfy these people anymore. Nor did they seem to like the Islamic idea in the Koran of enjoying the company of beautiful virgins forever in paradise but no corporeal contact allowed. That would be a kind of hell for me.

If the human race was that driven to gather in death cafés to discuss what lies beyond the grave, I decided my own weird ideas on that topic might not sound too far-fetched. I can promise you, dear reader, that with my way, or rather nature's way, if you are a gardener or farmer, when your heart stops beating and you have to stop weeding, you can keep on feeding the soil indefinitely, no Twitter about it. As your body decomposes and folds back into the eternal garden of the food chain, your loved ones will think all the more kindly of you, if for no other reason than at least you will be doing them the favor of not keeping on tweeting.

I write this book believing that the human race, including myself, is irrational. But being irrational is not all that bad. Winter aconites, merrily blooming yellow above a sudden carpet of spring snow, are rather irrational, but the effect is, well, very nice. Human irrationality is extremely un-nice only because humans are genetically predisposed toward violence, a particularly lethal kind of irrationality. Whenever two or more people gather together, they will eventually start killing each other, and even if there were only one human remaining, he or she would probably commit suicide for lack of anyone else to kill. What makes this so maddening is that each and every one of these genetically predisposed killers will strive to do anything to stay alive and to protect, at the risk of their own lives, other people who are not at the moment a threat to them. The whole cultural history of human activity is a true story about people killing with one hand and saving lives with the other.

This dichotomy gives me hope that a human genotype will eventually evolve that is not capable of killing its own kind, but that would be a miracle, and believing in miracles is another kind of insanity. Nevertheless, totally contradicting everything I have written above (another mark of human insanity), I really do intend this book to be a comfort and a solace for those people facing death. And that means all of us.

CHAPTER 1

---·---

Impermanent Pastures

I don't know exactly when I began to question what I was taught about life and death, cause and effect, beginnings and endings, finiteness and infinity, permanence and impermanence, but I know when my doubts finally came to a head. Forty years ago I chose to come back to the scenes of my childhood and live out my life. The strip of land I settled on was along the banks of what the old maps call Warpole Creek, after a Wyandot Indian chief who had lived in the vicinity. The creek, which is hardly five feet wide and a foot deep except in flood times, connects my land to my childhood home place about two miles upstream, and the intervening valley of several hundred acres was my playground as a boy and my education as a man. For over a century, sheep kept this small valley bounded by low but rather steep hills as smooth a sward of grass as a golf course. I could roam over it at will because the land all belonged to members of my mother's family, the Ralls. I did not appreciate my good fortune. I took it for granted. Couldn't everyone roam freely over hundreds of acres of private parkland?

Even as children, we called it "permanent pasture," the two words running together in our minds as if they were one—*permanentpasture*. That's what our farmer parents called it. In our minds, it had always been pastureland and always would be.

I should have figured out from the land itself that permanency is a false concept. For one thing, there were huge old stumps rotting away in these pastures denoting a woodland past, remnants of which still dotted the permanent pasture here and there. For another, there was a prehistoric earthwork rearing up right where St. James Run flows into Warpole Creek. (How about that—a European Jewish-Christian name colliding with a Native American name in the depths of an Ohio sheep pasture.) At least everyone said it was a human-built mound. It stood out peculiarly alone, unconnected to the valley slopes that ran along the creek. I was totally captivated by it and read every book about the "Mound Builders" that our local library carried. I knew these mystery people were not the Wyandot and Delaware Indians who were living here before us. I would stand on top of the pear-shaped mound and imagine those mysterious people carrying basketfuls of dirt to the site like the books said they did. I pretended I was one of them, a throwback to their culture. I tried to will them into existence, demanding that they rise up out of the earth and speak to me. Was there a reason they erected the mound right there at the conjunction of the two creeks? Was it even then the best fishing hole in the valley?

To make matters even more mysterious, on the brow of the valley hills across Warpole Creek from my home place stood an abandoned well pipe around which the ground was strewn with pieces of pottery, evidence that a pioneer American home had once stood there. My sister, who with her husband eventually built a new home close by, found a gold wedding ring on the site. What made these artifacts of our culture so jarring was that sometimes we could find right among them flint arrowheads of much older civilizations. Family folklore claimed that a black man who worked for our grandfather had lived there in a shack. But obviously a family had lived there and it had been in earlier times more than a mere shack. These people, however, were as mysterious to us as the ones who built the mound. Mom called the pieces of pottery strewn across the ground "china." China was as far away to us as the Mound Builders.

Our family's first reaction to the mound was to desecrate it. One of my old uncles told me that Great-Grandfather plowed it up and grew corn on it one time, something that might be possible with horses and a single-bottom plow, but hardly with a tractor because three of the slopes were too steep. I tended not to believe my uncle until he pointed out to me the old dead furrows still plainly visible on the steep grassy hillsides across the creek from the mound. If those hills could be plowed, I suppose the mound could be, too. But why would the early settlers have planted steep hillsides when there was level, rich bottomland nearby? Probably because the level ground had to be cleared of huge trees and tile-drained before it could be farmed.

The marks on the land kept telling me plainly enough that this valley was anything but permanent pasture. It only became pasture because the early farmers finally could see that the valley hillsides, though rather low, were too steep for constant cultivation, and some of the level land next to the creek was too swampy and prone to flooding. Besides, every farm needed pasture for cows and sheep back then, so turning the slopes into pasture made good economic sense. Economics ruled, of course.

When I came back to my beloved childhood playground in 1975, it was still pasture and a few tree groves, dotted with cows and sheep. I was so happy to see my son and daughter romp over this meadow in summer and zip down the hills on sleds in winter, just as I had done. The continuity bulwarked my treasured sense of permanence. I had left other previous residences, in Minnesota, Indiana, and Pennsylvania, when new houses came marching into view on the horizon. I had nightmares, now, about subdivisions swarming over these home pastures.

But from the time I returned home, except for our few acres and a few more that my brothers-in-law owned at the other end of our old playground, the "permanent pasture" was giving way to another kind of impermanence I had never reckoned on. It was slowly being abandoned both by industrial, mechanized grain farmers and by livestock farmers. The sheer size of modern machinery made it uneconomical to cultivate and harvest these sloping hillsides and small creekside valleys. Nor was the amount of land large enough to encourage profitable livestock grazing operations in the get-big-or-get-out era of farming. Aiding the abandonment, government programs paid farmers for not cultivating or pasturing stream-bank land. So these pastures slowly began to revert to forest. I have watched, fixated and awed, for nearly forty years, as the meadows turned into a mass of weeds and brush. By 2013, tree saplings were gaining ascendancy. If a Wyandot Indian had gone to sleep in the woodland along Warpole Creek in 1870 and awakened like Rip Van Winkle in 2070, he would probably notice no difference in the landscape around him, except perhaps for the bones of great metal farm machines rotting away like dinosaurs among the trees.

The change was so gradual that for a decade I hardly realized what was happening. Then I wanted to buy up that land but could not afford to do so. A day came when the growth of weeds and brush was so thick that I could not even walk through it. On hands and knees I crawled under it, sometimes breaking into tears, mourning the days of my youth. It only slowly dawned on me that nature was just doing what nature was supposed to do, returning these pastures to woodland again. What was happening was not something bad. Only in my mind was it a cause for tears.

But I have at least learned not to predict what will happen next too hastily. Impermanence could take a different turn. Perhaps in another hundred years or so, a "new" kind of farming will return, and young "pioneers" will again clear the land and graze livestock here. Or maybe turn these old hills into a golf course. That is not as preposterous as it sounds. On the level field above the valley, hardly a thousand feet from the mound, a landing strip for airplanes called Rall Field flourished for a brief time in the 1930s. In those days, there were many grandiose notions about the future of flying—an airplane in every barn. My great-uncle worked his pencil stub on the daybook he kept in the front pocket of his bib overalls and decided, especially after a plane nosed down into another dratted old dead furrow and crumpled up like an accordion, that corn paid better than airstrips.

How had I come by the foolish notion of permanency, and, by extension, of immortality, of infinity, of limitless space, all of which are beyond the comprehension of the human mind? I could grasp, sort of, the concepts of mortal life, impermanent pastures, limited borders, and time that measures events with beginnings and endings. But why was I cursed with a brooding sense of everlastingness, of permanent pastures? Other animals live only in the present, unwittingly following a kind of wisdom that took me eighty years to appreciate and would probably take me eighty more to acquire. My black hen can sing her querulous, clucky-lucky song of contentedness all day long because she has no notion of old earthworks almost visible from her coop, or dead furrows scarring hillsides that should never have been plowed, or flint arrows possibly lying in the ground right under her feet, or that maybe in the next few minutes she will die under the talons of a hawk. I listen to her with envy because for me mortal danger has always lurked around every corner. I sing mostly sad songs and keep one eye fixed over my shoulder. Could I ever convince myself what the hen knows: There is no beginning or ending in the real world but only the forever NOW.

This is not just whimsy-whamsy, idle philosophizing. Everywhere you look today you see brilliant minds trying to explain infinity, trying very hard to explain away an idea that we are cursed to carry around with us but cannot grasp. The Higgs boson, for instance. If this boson talk were coming from ordinary, everyday humans, we would all laugh at their vanity. But it comes from canonized intellectuals, otherwise known as scientists. They suspect that there is something to this infinity business and believe it is their duty to try to explain it as it relates to "space." They invent new words. Naming something gives it identity and therefore seems to give it definition. We can almost believe that we have concrete knowledge about the infinity of space because we can now pronounce the word *boson* and put it in a place, in this case a Higgs "field." A boson is a subatomic particle and by definition has no size. Right away red flags go up in my brain, especially since the Higginites are now arguing about whether they really did discover it yet, as the news exclaimed recently. In trying to describe this strange boson to poor ignorant folk, the Higginites resort to amazingly imaginative metaphors. One writer I found online likens a boson to a pure white snowflake in a blizzard of pure white snowflakes, falling on an unlimited blanketing landscape of pure white snowflakes. Another describes the Higgs "field" where bosons roam as "dark energy" in an "invisible mist." Another tries to make bosons intelligible by alluding to windblown dust sifting off a wall—but the wall isn't really there. This is the kind of horse manure language that poets and theologians are fond of. I'm actually fond of it myself. But I surely can't accept deductions drawn from it as fact, especially when the thing with no size hasn't indisputably been found yet. I think maybe bosons are angels. I wonder how many of them can dance on the head of a pin. The scientists involved don't like it, but the Higgs boson is being called the "God particle." Perfect. Science is trying to identify and define infinite intelligence. It is trying to reinvent God.

Or what about the latest discovery from the far reaches of space? Our telescopes have discovered the so-called Phoenix Cluster, which contains hundreds of thousands of galaxies. The galaxies are throwing off seven hundred stars every year, so we are told. The size of even one galaxy is beyond the embrace of the human mind. Hundreds of thousands of them in a "cluster," chucking out stars like a pitching machine chucks out baseballs, is, literally, unthinkable. Trying to grasp bosons and Phoenix Clusters and dark energy and invisible mist, I wonder whether those who believe in science are not just as gullible as those who believe in a God regulating it all. Perhaps the most gullible are those who believe in both.

My quandary finally almost resolved itself with a solution that both religion and science reject. Perhaps matter, or the material universe, or whatever you want to call "it," is eternal. "It" had no beginning and will never end. That idea satisfied much of my puzzlement over both religion and science, though it contradicted the former's insistence on a God-Creator and the latter's insistence that every natural effect must have a natural cause. I no longer had to worry about how it all began and how it all will end.

I thought, standing on the Indian mound in my little valley, that I had come up with a new idea about The Meaning of It All, only to find that it had been voiced in Taoism at least six hundred years before Christianity came on the scene, and if the archaeologists are correct, most likely before my mound came into existence. And the notion has been repeated many times since. I just hadn't read the right books. It is not easy to find the right books because my newfound notion contradicted religion's insistence on a God-Creator and science's insistence that every natural effect must have a natural cause. Neither explained to my satisfaction how everything got started as well as my seemingly preposterous notion that there was no beginning. Besides, that conclusion, if I dare speak of conclusions at all with my new way of thinking, had the singular effect of not just solving my mental quandaries about infinity, but helping me begin to lose my fear of death. It seemed to me that it is fear of death that prompts the human mind to look into far-off spaces it can't imagine and find there a kind of immortality it can't imagine, either. Once one decides that there is no such thing as death but only a change in life-form, the clutching paranoid fear of it begins to fade.

What happened next was that I suddenly found myself facing death. Really, not hypothetically. Cancer. Marking time became simply a matter of marking the number of chemotherapy treatments before remission would or would not occur. What I had only haltingly been arriving at in my mind about immortality now began to bolster my spirit. I went from fear to anger to numbness, and finally to an almost calm realization that contemplating death was as much a waste of time as trying to count dark energy or wondering when Warpole Creek Valley will again be cleared for pasture.

Strangely, however, I did not study Taoism, where I had found the philosophical roots of my new notion of life everlasting. I studied my garden and my farm instead. I hunkered down into my little bit of nature even more than I had before. The answer, at least enough answer to keep me from despair, was right there in front of my eyes. The natural world had been trying to tell me what I needed to know all along, but I had allowed the voices from the unnatural and the supernatural worlds to drown it out. Sitting in my garden, almost too weak to reach down and pull weeds, I could face death almost peacefully because I had come to realize that the garden, as part of the whole earth-garden, was eternal. As part of earth-garden, I was part of the eternal. That's all the paradise I could stand to contemplate.

Chapter 2

Garden Therapy Along with Chemotherapy

I have a notion that it is a little easier for gardeners and farmers to accept death than the rest of the populace. Every day we help plants and animals begin life and help plants and animals end life. We are acculturated to the food chain. We understand how all living things are seated around a dining table, eating while being eaten. We realize that all of nature is in flux. I work in all seasons on a strawberry patch that for only three weeks produces fruit. All year Carol cares for a patch of irises that bloom in magnificent glory for hardly two weeks. The amaryllis plant sits in somnolence in its pot in the basement all winter, then suddenly awakens in March and puts forth two unimaginably beautiful blossoms. In just ten days the flowers fade and the show is over for another year. This is reality; this is the fact of life and the fact of death that is so hard to accept.

Shepherds spend night and day in early spring playing midwife to ewes, sometimes working desperately through the night to save lambs from dying at birth. Kneeling in manure and afterbirth with your arm up to its elbow inside a ewe is hardly fun. Then all summer the ewes and lambs must be watched and wormed and protected from maggots and wolves and coyotes and the neighbors' damned dogs. Why do we do it? It's certainly not for money, because most of us don't make much as shepherds. But when those lambs go bouncing across the green spring pasture, all the pain and suffering that got them there is forgotten and the shepherd rejoices. Then comes autumn, and those lambs upon which one has spent so much labor and love are shipped off to the stockyards and to death. A friend, a farmer all his life, tells me a story that brings tears to his eyes. Once, after he had hauled his steers off to the stockyards, he stayed to watch them sell. The large building in which the animals from each farmer were penned separately until they were auctioned off had a catwalk above it from which the animals could all be viewed. My friend went up there to look at his charges one last time, and as he talked with another farmer, his steers recognized his voice, lifted their heads, and bawled at him piteously. "They heard me. They were crying out for me to save them," my friend says. "It just shook my soul."

I used to ask myself what kind of perversity drives us gardeners and farmers to settle for such a life, but it was only when I faced death from cancer that I could start to answer that question with any conviction. Carol had to do most of the gardening that spring because I was so weak. But sometimes between chemotherapy sessions, I had energy enough to sit in a chair and, seated, weed by hand and with hoe. Actually, pulling weeds or hoeing from a sitting position is not comfortable, so what I really did most of the time was get down on my hands and knees, pull a few weeds, use the chair to pull myself up, sit awhile to catch my breath, stand up and hoe a bit, and sit down and rest some more. Working this way forced me into a very close relationship with the life around me. One of the first tasks that I set out to accomplish was to clean up the black raspberry patch, which had been neglected for a year. Instead of roaring down between rows with the tiller or hacking vigorously along with the hoe, always in a hurry, I was sort of enclosed within the raspberry vines, which had spread out from the original rows and seemed more like a little jungle than a garden. I could only weed or hoe or prune the vines closest to the chair, then pick up the chair and advance a little farther along. I had to step on some of the vines, or push them out of the way or get entwined within them. I was, in other words, in close communion with raspberrydom.

Being that close to the plants for long periods of time, I became very aware of a whole kaleidoscope of natural life around me, much of which I had never really focused on before. I expected to find the perverse chickweed, the cursed sow thistle, and the stubborn dandelion, but where on earth did that lovely dill plant come from? Could I just leave it to grow there? (Yes—when you are weak, companion planting of just about anything suddenly works fine.) And what was this strange grass that was spreading so rapidly over the ground? It looked a little like bluegrass until it went to seed, which it did in what seemed like three hours. In fact I counted nineteen different kinds of weeds under the raspberry plants. This was in an area of about fifteen feet wide by thirty feet long. One of them was bedstraw. Where on earth had that come from?

Tree seedlings were gaining a firm toehold, too, much to my dismay. A raspberry patch, at least the way I manage one with leaf mulch, becomes a tree nursery heaven, especially when located next to a tree grove. In just one year of not weeding, there were at least a score of white ash seedlings and a dozen black walnut seedlings that had popped up under the berry vines. That's how I learned that the fervor for planting trees à la Arbor Day rituals is mostly unnecessary. If there are trees anywhere in the vicinity, just lay down a foot of leaf mulch where you want more to grow and stand back. The trees will come, believe me. There were several two-year-old ash seedlings among the raspberry canes that, because I had not had the opportunity to sit still among the vines, I had missed the previous year. They were five feet tall already and growing above the berry vines! A transplanted seedling will never grow that fast.

These seedlings were telling me something else. Just because all the old white ash trees were dying out from emerald ash borer depredation, it did not mean the end of the white ash. Seedlings were growing all over the place, and they will continue to grow, like elm seedlings had done, to seed-bearing age before the emerald ash borer can wipe them out. The ash borer, like the elm beetle, will run out of big trees to feed on and be so drastically reduced in numbers that the young trees will start producing seed for more trees before the borer can kill them.

That's when the thought hit me. In nature, nothing much really dies. The various life-forms renew themselves. *Renewal*, not *death*, is the proper word for the progression of life in nature. If I died of cancer, the proper response would be to bury my flesh and bones for fertilizer in a celebration of natural renewal.

During much of the time spent out among the berry vines, I just sat in my chair, not working at all. This led to another fascinating discovery. The berry vines were in blossom, and shortly I noticed that a remarkable variety of insects were visiting those blooms and spreading pollen. There were first of all honeybees and bumblebees. This was very significant to me because I had thought that we'd lost our honeybees. Everywhere you looked, agricultural news reports were singing a requiem for the honeybee. Yet obviously there were still some wild hives in tree holes in the woods. This was a cause for rejoicing in itself, because we are surrounded by very widespread and active chemical spray farming, which is said to be the cause of the decline. Despite so much hand-wringing in garden and farm magazines and books about the dearth of honeybees, and in some cases bumblebees, our bees had escaped all the new diseases and adverse chemicals that were threatening them. Lesson to be learned: Don't overreact to bad news, including cancer.

Then I began to notice all the other bugs flying from one raspberry blossom to another. They were obviously not just out for the exercise or to admire the scenery. They were sipping nectar in most cases and in the process they had to be spreading pollen. Maybe only a little, but some. In all the worrisome talk about losing our pollinating bees, this observation was extremely pertinent. I was aware of the progress being made to develop orchard mason bees as pollinators. You can actually buy them now, along with "hives" to raise them in (they are actual solitary, stingless bees); Territorial Seed Company is the source I know. But the point was that obviously there were other pollinators out there working away, though not often publicized. Excitedly, I started making a list, pencil and pad at hand, trusty insect guide in my lap. I felt that I was making a major discovery, at least for myself, and in the process of getting excited by that, I didn't think about dying from cancer for hours on end.

The most surprising insect pollinating the raspberries was a gaudy moth, an eight-spotted forester, mostly black with two white spots on each hind wing, dazzling orange-red forelegs, and a bright yellow spot on each forewing. It had a wingspan of about an inch and a quarter, so it was quite startling and easy to follow with the eye. And of course bugs are so much easier to approach closely than birds, so watching them was more satisfying. The bug book mentioned what the larva fed on but not a word about the moth eating anything. It is commonly believed that many moths eat nothing during their short lives, but if this one was not supping on the nectar in the cusp of the flower, I'd surely like to know what it was doing.

The other colorful pollinator was the red admiral butterfly. Again the bug book spoke only of how its caterpillar feeds mainly on hops and nettles. Not a word about what the butterfly eats, if anything. This one fluttered from one raspberry blossom to another, burying its head down inside the petals, obviously sipping nectar. I doubt it was collecting very much pollen to take to another blossom, but some surely.

The real eye-openers in this pollination business were a couple of bees I knew next to nothing about previously: the virescentgreen metallic bee and the augochloragreen metallic bee. They are smaller than honeybees, and their bodies are mostly a shiny metallic green in color as the names indicate. They were working the raspberry blossoms in earnest, crawling down among the stamens to get to the nectar, in the process brushing up lots of pollen on their legs. They were obviously effective pollinators. The bug book (I use *The Audubon Society Field Guide to Insects and Spiders* because it has lots of pictures and was relatively inexpensive) describes how these bees depend on pollen to raise their larvae as much as honeybees do. They are prettier than honeybees, too, and don't sting.

Quite a few silver-spotted skippers frequented the raspberry blossoms. They were after nectar, too. We usually see them on zinnias later in the year. Also flitting about was a tiny gray butterfly and some tiny, brilliantly colored gnat-like insects that I was unable to identify. Several ladybug beetles happened by. I presume they were looking for aphids. But a shiny blue fly, a blue bottle fly as far as I could ascertain, also visited the flowers. The book says they feed on rotting meat. But then, consulting more books, I learned that in some insect species, the male and female feed quite differently. Female mosquitoes are the ones that sting for blood. The males, yep, sip nectar. Male horseflies drink nectar. It is the females who so plague the livestock. Maybe with bottle flies, only one sex likes rotten meat. Or maybe both like a little nectar for dessert. There was so much I didn't know, so much to discover just sitting in a chair in a garden.

I was surprised to find several black and yellow mud daubers flitting from flower to flower. And a bald-faced hornet. Surely they did not drink nectar, I thought. But the books assured me that they did. In fact a surprising number of insects sip nectar for sustenance. The ones without bristles on their legs probably don't transfer much pollen from flower to flower, but they almost have to move some and since, as I was learning, there are so many of them, their activity is bound to provide some pollination. And why should that surprise me? Honeybees are not native to America. Obviously, nature here got along just fine without them. The biggest pollinator in nature is the wind. I decided that much of our worry about nature these days was paranoia stemming from incomplete knowledge. Most likely true of cancer, too.

The raspberries quit blooming long before I had learned all there was to learn about pollinating insects. It might be that the body of knowledge on the subject is nearly limitless. I am convinced that one could spend a lifetime sitting there in the garden and learn only a little of all that is going on there. Under the umbrella of therapy, a curious mind, without one mile of travel or travail, could become the next E. O. Wilson.

The excitement I was experiencing in the garden, even when weakened by chemotherapy, encouraged a positive attitude in me that surely helped me deal with the cancer, but the effect went much farther than that. The garden therapy also kept alive my desire to keep on writing. I started joking that chemotherapy might have some kind of narcotic chemical in it that induced or increased creative urges. Plenty of writers believe some drugs do that for them. Some patients on chemo use medical marijuana to ease the discomfort. Some of the outrageously opaque poetry I read these days in *The New Yorker* makes me wonder if it is the result of combining chemo and pot.

I think cancer drove me to write more rather than less for the same reason that a fruit tree will increase output if its bark is lacerated with cuts and slashes. Threatened with danger, the writer as well as the apple tree is frightened into greater production. Pecking away on a keyboard does not require much physical energy, and my mind seemed to be just seething with deathbed drama. I have read about quite a few other writers who continued to write, frantically it seemed, till the day they died. (Is that accepting death or fighting it?) The secret of writing is to see everything, however common and nondescript, as drama, and certainly nothing is more dramatic than dying. We poor souls addicted to putting letters in rows across paper or electronic screens keep right on going, like a blind horse over a cliff. Dying is the best story we will ever cover, and the only sad part of it is that good writing requires experience in the subject, which is kind of hard to do with death.

Being able, being driven actually, to continue writing was wonderfully therapeutic for me, made even more so because the subject of my writing was mostly nature as it played out in gardening and farming, the great teachers of death acceptance. Who can say how much of this kind of therapy might have played a role in my recovery?

At any rate there came a day when we went, fearfully, into the doctor's office to hear the verdict after half a year of chemo. When we first entered the room, the main doctor had not arrived, but his assistant was wearing a wonderfully radiant smile on her face. It was not her job to tell us the details of my condition, but she didn't have to. All she said was that "we really have good news for you." And so it was. The cancer was in remission. I would still have to have a treatment every other month for two years, but it was not the chemo, just the stuff that sniffs out cancer cells that try to come back and kills them.

The docs figure I will probably go on now for a few more years anyway and die of something else, perhaps an irate Republican. For sure it won't be my old Corriedale ram who has tried to kill me several times. I got rid of him before he could do it to me.

A day later, Carol and I were back home after three hours of heavy traffic, which I hate almost as much as cancer. Surrounded by the peacefulness of home, I felt like I had died and gone to heaven, especially after a double shot of bourbon, which was tasting good again. It was May, my favorite month. The lawns, in need of mowing, were a magnificent carpet of yellow dandelions and purple violets. The whole tree grove around us was in magnificent glory. We opened the mail, always the first thing we do on coming home after letting out the hens if our son hasn't already done so. Among the bills there was a royalty check for somewhat more money than what we were used to getting. Carol and I looked at each other triumphantly. There was that wonderful glow of happiness back in her eyes. I was tempted to think in that precious moment that maybe the cancer had almost been worth it just to make me appreciate how great my life has been. And it wasn't over yet.

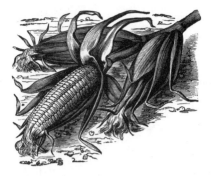

---◆---

CHAPTER 3

How Long Is Forever?

I was nine years old when I almost grasped how long forever lasts. I was feeding supplemental corn to the hogs that were grazing in a field across the road from our farmstead in the valley of Warpole Creek. The idea was to carry the corn in two 5-gallon buckets, one in each hand. But I had made a little game out of it. I would rank ears of corn on my left arm, balancing the first one at the crook of my elbow, then add ears down my arm to my fingertips. A second layer went on top of the first, in the indentations between the ears on the first layer and building up more layers in pyramidal fashion until no more ears would fit or my arm gave out from the weight. It was more of a balancing act than a feat of strength. As I remember, my high score was nineteen ears. (At age eighty, one remembers a whole lot more from age nine than from age seventy-nine.) On this particular day, my balancing act went awry and the ears spilled off onto the ground before I could steady them with my right hand.

"Dammit," I said. It was my first uttered cuss word, not to be taken lightly. In my very Catholic upbringing, cussing was a sin, at least for a little boy in 1940. (Men could cuss, and even my saintly mother could say "shit," another mystery I never did figure out.) I was not too worried, however, because I was already clever at maneuvering the loopholes of church dogma. Cussing was only a venial sin. Had it been a mortal sin and I died before I could get to a priest and confess my waywardness, I would go straight to hell. Going to hell was a big deal because it lasted forever.

Normally, I reacted to this kind of religious teaching the way most boys do. I heard it like I heard katydids and cicadas dinning the silence of an August afternoon with their incessant buzzing. The sounds of the words were there, part of the cultural environment, but not in any meaningful, cognitive way. But for some reason, at this particular moment, my mind focused on the concept of an eternal hell and I was overwhelmed with fright. Hell lasted forever. There was no end to it. Oh . . . my . . . God. *No end.* If everyone really understood how long everlasting fire lasted, no one would ever commit a mortal sin. The risk was just too terrible. I quivered a bit with the awful, unimaginable realization of how long forever lasted. And for the next year or so I suffered a scrupulous fear of going to hell. I made sure I didn't murder anyone, didn't rob a bank, didn't even do a "bad thing," which was my euphemism for masturbation, a word I didn't know yet. But I knew it was bad because those things down there between my legs were hot stuff. It was a sin to think about them.

"But how can you not think about them?" I asked the priest.

"You do not dwell on them."

"But if I try really hard not think about them, that just means I'm thinking about them all the harder, doesn't it?"

"You must learn to turn your attention elsewhere. There are so many more interesting subjects of contemplation."

"Oh."

Now, as I glared at the recalcitrant ears of corn, I remembered a talk our parish priest gave us a few years earlier. He was fairly immortal by that time himself, and spoke to us in words full of

Germanic butcherings of English consonants, a result of being born in what everyone still called "the old country." He knew how to talk to children very well, however. "You want to know how long eternity lasts?" he asked us from the front of the classroom. "Imagine a wery hard rock as big as the whole world. Now imagine a leetle bird landing dere once effrey million years to sharpen its beak. By da time dat rock would be worn away to nutting, eternity would be chust beginning." Now, staring at the damned ears of corn that didn't want to balance on my arm, I applied that description of eternity to hell instead of to heaven as I previously had done. No one deserved that, not even Hitler.

After that, I started noticing how blithely other children in school reacted to the awful vision of everlasting hellfire. They took in the words of religious dogma from the nuns while their attention was fixed on more important matters, like Martha Peabody's suddenly swelling breasts, or when the recess bell was going to ring, or if George Smith really was going to beat the crap out of Joey Kudz as he had promised yesterday. The religious teachings simply didn't register in their minds seriously as far as I could tell, yet many of them would go on believing strange notions to their dying day—like Mary, the Mother of God, giving birth to another God, or maybe the same one, even though she was a virgin. And then instead of actually dying, she was carried up, up, and away into heaven by angels. I might have been somewhat innocent about the definition of virginity, but being a country boy I knew that a cow could not have a calf unless there was a bull around somewhere. Angels seemed a bit mysterious, too. Sort of like Superman and Santa Claus. But while everybody seemed to understand that Superman and Santa Claus were make-believe, they all believed firmly in guardian angels, especially the one that somehow persuaded George Smith not to beat the crap out of Joey Kudz.

I would torment my poor mother with my doubts.

"Sister Mary Francis says that God always was and always will be," I might say as an opener.

"Yesssss." She would nod, wariness already creeping into her voice.

"Then how could he have had a mother?"

"His son had a mother."

"But the son was God, too, right? Sister said so." The words of nuns carried a whole lot more weight to me than what the pope said.

"Welllll, yessss."

"How could God have a mother if he had no beginning and no end?"

"It's all a mystery. You must have faith. Shouldn't you be in the barn doing your chores?"

What saved me from worrying over these mysteries too much was that I would grow tired of dwelling on any particular quandary, always able to find a new one to occupy my mind. After awhile, even the idea of hellfire got boring.

CHAPTER 4

Killdeer Woman

I don't know how many times we told her not to climb up into the haymow to throw down hay for her calves. But Mother wouldn't listen. She never listened to people telling her to take it easy. People had been telling her for years not to carry heavy buckets of feed to the chickens when she was pregnant; not to hoe her garden when her back hurt; not to get up at 5 AM to help with the milking when her kidney infection flared up. She paid no attention. She was contemptuous of physical weakness—and mental weakness, too. She would never let her children mope around feeling sorry for themselves. "When you grow up and get some real problems, you'll think you deserve the luxury of a nervous breakdown," she would tell us. And then she'd give us more work to do.

So there she went, all alone, up into the mow again, probably singing (she was always singing), and at fifty-eight she could climb a barn ladder as spryly as a seventeen-year old. But something happened this time. No one will ever know how, but somewhere along the edge of the mow she lost her balance and fell. Fell and broke her neck. Broke her neck and died.

But it didn't happen all that fast. She was too tough for that. She lay in the manure, unable to move or cry out. Father found her there with our dog licking her face. She whispered that Tillie licking her in the face felt good.

Even to this day many years later, I can barely force myself to think about it. I didn't know how Father could take it. I could not bear the thought of it. I wanted to hold my father in my arms and love away the memory. But he stood it. And my brother stood it. And my seven sisters stood it. Because Mother had taught us that you could stand anything when you had to.

In the hospital, the doctors put a pin in her head and attached a weight to it so her neck would not move. She complained only that they took away her false teeth, which none of us children knew she had worn for twenty years. Her head had to be shaved and, ugly as that seemed to make her appear, for the first time I could tell how very much she looked like her father.

He had never given up, either. When he was eighty-four, he demolished his pickup truck and walked away unhurt. After that the family would not let him drive from his house in town to his farm right outside the village. So he walked. By the time he was ninety, he'd become confused, walk the wrong way, and get lost. They forbade him to leave the house. So he'd sneak out. Finally they took his shoes away from him. That was the only way they could keep him off his land.

And I remembered Ed Hesse, the old Minnesota farmer whom I worked for as a hired man. When he lay dying, shot through with cancer and other diseases, no one of which was enough to kill him, to the very end he kept sliding his good leg out from under the covers and banging it against the bed rail. "See," he'd say. "I still got one part of me in good shape."

And so now, my mother. She lay in the hospital a week, refusing to give up. She was paralyzed from the waist down, but wouldn't admit it.

"Look, Gene," she'd say. "See how I can move my hands. See how strong my grip is." And I'd have to put my finger into the palm of her hand and she would try to grasp it. She could not turn her head to see that her hand, which had held nine children growing up, which had gripped countless hoe handles and pitchforks and tractor steering wheels, which had pulled milk from who knows how many cow teats, could not now hold on to even my slack finger.

But she kept working at it, flexing her arms all day, all night. We could tell when she was conscious that way. Her hands would quiver, clench, open, clench. Even when she had no strength to talk, her fingers kept up the fight.

Finally she announced to all of us that she had given herself a goal. By the time daughter Rosy had her baby in the spring, she'd be able to sit in a wheelchair and hold it in her arms, she declared. She kept repeating that. It is the very last thing she said to me.

But that is not the end of the story. Old farmers, like old soldiers, never die. They stamp a piece of land with an indomitable spirit that lives forever. This is how I know.

There were long gray days after the burial, days too hard to recall, when about the only thing that kept us going were those words of hers that had kept us going before. "When you get some real problems, you'll think you deserve the luxury of a nervous breakdown." I was traveling extensively then from our home in the Philadelphia suburbs. Always before, I could lift a telephone in Chicago or St. Louis or wherever and call home and she would be there. So now I tried to call down those long, lonesome wires of the traveler and no one would answer. Father was living there, but he was always someplace working. Sisters were around, but they were always out. And that is how I finally came to accept Mother's death. She was not at home anymore to answer the phone.

A day came when I could go back to the cemetery. It was early spring in the flat Ohio country with only a little greening to it. I walked to the grave, prepared to have the sorrow all plowed up again. I was thinking about how deaf and dumb cemeteries were, the eerie display of granite and flowers and live people standing over bones becoming earth again. And maybe that feeling of distraught desperation prepared me for what I found on Mother's grave because what I found bears not the scrutiny of logic.

What did I find? A bird, a killdeer, sitting on a nest of eggs, on top of Mother's grave. The bird fluttered away at my approach, screaming in defense of her brood, pretending that she was hurt, trying to lure the intruder away from the life it was her life to protect.

Mother always loved killdeers—she called our farm Killdeer Place. I had to smile. Ignoring the tombstone, I stooped to examine the eggs. Infuriated, the killdeer charged me. She held off, an arm's length away, seeming to stamp her foot the very way Mother used to do when she was angry. My sudden unbidden laugh rang out over the quiet cemetery. My children, who were with me, did not understand. They saw a bird and three eggs in the grass. I saw the spirit of my mother, screaming in defense of creation, turning even her grave into a green cradle of life.

CHAPTER 5

Marble Orchards Can Be Fruit Orchards, Too

We called cemeteries "marble orchards" when I was growing up. I thought that was hilarious the first time or two around. Later, I came to realize that *orchard* could be a rather appropriate word for a graveyard. Many cemeteries are really marvelous groves of trees. When our cemeteries were started years ago, at least out in rural areas, few farmers and even townspeople thought they had the time or money to invest in exotic and decorative plants around their houses. But everyone was in favor of turning the homes of the dead into veritable arboretums. Also, because the homes of the dead were honored as sacred places, never to be molested, they became, and remain, preserves not only of unusual ornamentals but also of exotic wild native plants that elsewhere were being destroyed by farming and industry.

One of the most dramatic examples of how cemeteries can preserve and protect the environment I saw while accompanying

Wendell Berry on a walk across his home stomping grounds to see a little old abandoned pioneer cemetery. Wendell had a reason for taking me there but did not tell me what it was. He didn't have to. The tiny cemetery, hardly an acre in size, stood all alone out in a field that had been cultivated for over a century. It really "stood out," a good five feet above the surrounding field's surface. That is how much erosion had taken place around the protected island of gravestones. I didn't notice any rare, native plants from the past that could have been growing there because I was not at the time aware of that possibility. But for sure the soil that the cemetery kept from being eroded away was virgin and teeming with microbial life that was absent from the bared subsoil around it. The cemetery soil might have been especially fertile for all those bodies having rotted away to humus there, since here at least the bodies would likely have been buried in wooden coffins only, rather than encased in sealed vaults as would likely be the case now.

The combination of protected virgin soil, unusual or exotic landscape plants, and occasionally native pioneer species in a cemetery can act like a magnet, drawing a rich array of wildlife to the shelter of the lifeless stones. Far from being merely graveyards, these sanctuaries are gardens, and, with a little extra effort, could be very productive and instructive gardens teeming with as much life aboveground as there are bones below ground.

A good example of what can happen occurred recently in Oak Hill cemetery just a couple of miles from my home. There are many old hemlock trees growing there. Hemlocks are not native to this area, and no doubt that's why they were planted many years ago—something extra special to honor the dead. Hemlocks old enough to bear seed profusely are even rarer in these parts. In the winter of 2009 bird-watchers found that the trees were alive with white-winged crossbills, a bird that is rarely seen this far south. Crossbills feed on hemlock seed, which is normally plentiful in their arboreal feeding and nesting grounds up in Canada. Their beaks are actually crossed, which enables them to separate the seeds easily from the cones. Ornithologists believe the birds came south looking for food when their usual hemlocks in the northern forests did not bear many cones. For awhile, Oak Hill had an unusual influx of human visitors, too, as bird-watchers came from all over, even from other states, to see the rare sight. White-winged crossbills are fun to watch because they do not fear humans as much as most other birds, possibly because, in their far northern habitats, they do not often see humans and so have not learned to fear us. Up in the hemlock trees they were almost invisible, but many cones had fallen and the birds flocked to the ground to feed. I could walk right up to within ten feet of them and they seldom flew—just hopped a few more feet away.

What made the incident uncannily comforting to me was that all this was happening there on top of the bones of old acquaintances, friends, and ancestors. Wittingly or unwittingly, by making cemeteries botanically beautiful, society gathered in the living to keep company with the dead in a sort of ongoing dance of everlasting life. The cemetery had become something of an eternal garden.

I love to visit cemeteries. First of all, they are usually accessible without special permission. Second, they are almost always peaceful places where one can find restful solitude. I check out the nooks and crannies and border fences that might shelter rare prairie plants in places lawn mowers can't reach. Often I go to burial grounds to trace histories of particular families or to look for old gravestones that display examples of folkloric art. Grave markers are records of legend as well as history. A woman buried in one of our local cemeteries was thought to have been murdered although no charge was ever made. The story got around that her image was emerging on the stone to haunt the suspected murderer. I naturally had to check that out. Sure enough, in the flickering flame of a cigarette lighter, the granite seams in the tombstone bore a resemblance to a woman's profile with her hair streaming out behind her. All one had to do was give imagination a free rein and it looked for sure as if the hair was actually ruffling in the wind. The "obstacle illusion," as one of my neighbors likes to say, was so vivid that people started flocking to the cemetery in such numbers that the stone had to be removed to avoid vandalism. What a shame. The stone and its folklore were doing what cemeteries should do: act as gathering places to keep alive the memory of the dead and a kind of lingering immortality—even for, perhaps especially for, murder victims.

A more practical way to conjure up immortality is sculpting statues of the departed. The Greeks turned this idea into an artistic manufacturing business. Surely Michelangelo made David immortal, even if David never actually existed. The tallest monument in our Oak Hill cemetery immortalizes David Harpster, a pioneer farmer who once drove sheep and cattle from here in Ohio to faraway cities like Baltimore and Philadelphia. He was such a successful cowboy that he became known as the Wool King of the World. He sold one of his many farms to pay for his cemetery statue and for hoisting it several stories high over his burial plot. If you know what you are looking at, you can see it from a mile away. I wave at him every time I go by, because Harpster, like me, was a very contrary farmer. To please his wife, he finally consented to be baptized in his later years. Folklore says that the preacher had to dunk him three times because the first two times he came up cussing.

Today's practice of having permanent photographs imprinted on tombstones is the modern form of statuary. I took my grandsons through Oak Hill cemetery one time, my intention being to acquaint them with some of their forebears. We came upon the tombstone of a young person whom they had known. There she was, almost real, staring out at us in a magnificent photo embedded in the stone. But instead of being comforted, the boys were unnerved and insisted on leaving the cemetery immediately.

Now, hungering for immortality, people install electronic devices into the tombstone's surface by some technologically magical process far beyond the understanding of mere writers like me. A visitor, I am told, can activate these records with a cell phone or similar contrivance and, on its screen, the buried person's history and photo and other memorabilia pop up.

When my grandsons were visibly shaken by seeing the image of a classmate on a tombstone, it made me wonder about the whole macabre, vain attempt to prolong the lives of loved ones. Such efforts are not really comforting to the living, but only disturbing. They do not produce contentment. It was like—and I will bet anything this will happen among those rich enough to afford it—fashioning a robot to look like a departed loved one and letting it continue to make that person's habitual rounds. I could drive by the old home place and see Mom weeding her garden. Creepy.

"Hi, Mom, how's it going?"

"I. Am. Not. Mom. I. Am. A. Robot."

She, I mean it, would have to be programmed to answer that way so as not to create confusion. Real people would have to use their smartphones to help them figure out whether the people walking past them down the street were dead or alive. Before long there would be whole retirement villages, or cemetery villages, where all those robots would live—I mean, walk around—at an enormous cost that, even if the wealthy paid 90 percent of their income in taxes, society could not afford.

I kept wondering. Wouldn't it be more comforting to accept the truth about how decomposition is the real way back to real life? Wouldn't it be more comforting to watch a tree grow over the bones of your mother? I would surely find more ease and contentment talking to a tree nurtured by her humus than to a robot or a statue or even a tombstone. Or how about making it possible for killdeers to build their nests in the grass over her body returning to humus? I have talked to killdeers in that situation and they have talked back.

One of my favorite songs is "Bury Me Out on the Lone Prairie." Now, as I thought about dual-purpose cemeteries, I also began to wonder exceedingly about burial itself. Who needs ornate coffins anyway? Imagine my embarrassment when I learned that dual-purpose cemeteries and simple interment in the ground were both very ongoing movements around the world. A significant number of people are opting for "green burial" or natural burial. In fact, there are quite a few businesses now catering to requests for burial in a shroud or a simple coffin constructed of materials like wicker and seagrass that decompose quickly in the soil. Exponents of the new burial rites cite statistics to show the wasteful cost and energy involved in traditional burial. Numbers vary, but per year we're talking something like 90,000 tons of steel caskets; 14,000 tons of steel vaults; 2,700 tons of bronze and copper caskets; 1,636,000 tons of reinforced concrete; and some 800,000 gallons of embalming fluid, which contains mostly formaldehyde, something that's toxic to natural soil microbes.

Many cultures have, in fact, gone this commonsense route. Orthodox Jews do not embalm their dead. Islamic law encourages burial in a simple shroud. In England there are now "farmers' fields cemeteries" where a field is set aside as part of the farm's diversified enterprises, offering people who want their bodies to decompose naturally in the soil a place to do so. Woodland sites are also coming into use for natural or eco-burial. The idea of one's body providing fertilizer for a tree is very popular.

Cynthia Beal, whom I was fortunate enough to meet through the miracle of the Internet, is one of the dedicated pioneers in this field. In 2004, she started the Natural Burial Company, which supplies everything for natural burial that you can think of and some I bet you can't think of, like woven fabric coffins that decompose readily in the soil. (Natural Burial Company is online of course.) When she started, Cynthia says, there were fifty-two entries on the subject on Google. By 2012 there were ninety-eight thousand and counting. She has now taken a position at Oregon State University, where she is developing a curriculum that will train students and professionals in sustainable cemetery management. "We want to collate the information and research from around the globe into a more coherent whole," she says. "Then we'll be able to build a bridge between cemetarians and those who can do the needed research. We will be able to get interns into cemetery work and train a new generation of managers, moving on from the usual city Parks Department blow-and-mow teams into habitat gardeners." She is also working on a book that she hopes to publish eventually titled *Be a Tree*. It explains all the multitudinous details and challenges that incorporating simple natural burial ideas into modern society entails.

When I allowed as how changing today's usual attitude toward burial was going to be a very slow cultural process, Cynthia disagreed. "I think it will come along fairly fast, say in twenty or thirty years. Economics alone will force a change. It is just too costly both to the pocketbook and the environment to keep on doing what we do now. Nor are religious attitudes necessarily an obstacle. Those who want to be buried this way often have a deep spirituality about it. And I've learned not to assume that Christians would oppose it. We get most of our calls asking for information or wanting to buy natural burial products from the Bible Belt."

She may be right. In my youth, cremation was not an option for Catholics. Now it is generally accepted. Cremation is, in fact, perceived by many people as kind of "natural" because so often the ash remains of the bodies are spread directly on some garden or farm or body of water that the deceased wanted them returned to. Sometimes the ashes, perhaps in a simple urn, perhaps directly into the ground, are buried in a deceased loved one's cemetery plot.

One of the earliest ways to slow down decomposition of dead bodies was mummification. The first mummies were the natural result of dry climates where decomposition was delayed naturally. Archaeologists theorize that burial was a practical way to avoid having lots of dead, dry cadavers cluttering up the landscape of very dry climates.

In religious orders in the Middle Ages (and in many older civilizations) monks seem to have decided that mummies were too much trouble and that it was more practical to let the flesh decompose and preserve the bones only. Whole rooms were devoted to housing skeletal remains. I try to imagine that kind of tradition today. Perhaps I could keep Mother's memory alive by having her skeleton ensconced in a chair in front of the TV— which would also serve as a snide comment about television fare.

Keeping skeletons around became as unhandy in the Middle Ages as keeping robots around today would be. Take the almost unbelievable tale of Pope Formosus in the waning years of the ninth century. He seems to have been a good enough fellow, but got caught up in the politics of the time, because the Vatican in those days was very much a political entity. The anti-Formosus faction got the poor man practically defrocked when he was a bishop, but then the pro-Formosus party reinstated him into official favor when they got in power and elected him pope. After he died, the other party seized control again, disinterred his remains, and with his regally clothed skeleton installed in the courtroom condemned him again, canceled all his official acts, and threw his bones in the Tiber. (I am not making any of this up.) Historically, the sentencing was called the Cadaver Synod. A monk retrieved the body from the river and buried it decently, so the story goes. When the pro-Formosus gang again took control, they hauled the poor skeleton into the limelight again and had it buried with all honors in St. Peter's Basilica in Rome, declaring all his official acts valid again. Unbelievably, when the other side returned to power, they disinterred his bones and be-skulled them! Old Formosus did not exactly gain immortality, but he came close. I can't wait until Hollywood discovers this story and makes him even more immortal.

In the meantime, I dream of the cemetery of the future, full of fruit and nut trees and ornamental plantings, some of which yield food, too, or holiday decorations like pinecones and bittersweet. At the entrance there would be a farmers' market to sell the surplus of food from the cemetery grounds. There might be wood for fuel or for carpentry from the trees that in time grow old and need to be replaced. I imagine a family picking up hickory nuts from Grand-mother's gravesite, remembering the pies she made from them. In the center of the grounds is a weather station, because a natural environment like that would give more accurate temperature records of the area than a weather station at an airport or rooftop. Bodies are buried with the utmost respect, but in ways that allow them to decompose quickly. Ashes from cremation spread over the grounds or buried shallowly would also add to soil fertility. And if a killdeer should build a nest on your mother's grave, well, is that not an infinitely better way to make her immortal?

CHAPTER 6

Oh, Those Glorious Keys to Eternal Life

*T*ype the words "keys to eternal life" into Google and up will pop over ten million results. Many of them are duplicates, of course, and most of them are preachments from various religions that go as far back as archaeologists can dig. But a surprising number of them are science-based theories and beliefs. When it comes to wishful thinking about eternal life, religion and science are much closer to each other philosophically than either camp wants to admit.

The almost everlasting number of "scientific" keys to everlasting life include: human cloning; eating lots of raw onions; consuming vast amounts of chocolate; practicing rejuvenation therapy; whole body transplants; incorporating into our DNA the "Methuselah gene," which Icelandic biotechnologists claim to have uncovered; indulging in lots of sexual orgasm; spending one's life in a protective plastic bubble; wearing an ANKH talisman from ancient

Egyptian times (whatever that is); trans-alchemy (whatever *that* is); stem cell research; a happy marriage; a happy family; copying how jellyfish, flatworms, and bacteria regenerate themselves; and cryogenics—freezing one's body at death so it can be thawed and reinvigorated when the key to eternal life is discovered. I labored my way through about three hundred entries of the ten million before I grew weary. Obviously, the number-one interest of the human race is how to live forever, even as we simultaneously kill one another off at colossal, genocidal rates.

Even as I write, another grand attempt at immortality is in the offing. The news is full of references to a Russian billionaire, Dmitry Itskov, who, with some thirty scientists, has launched "the 2045 Initiative," aimed at achieving human immortality in just thirty years' time. This resolute band of comrades-in-immortality is going to accomplish this goal by routinely upgrading humans (if they have enough money, or maybe Medicare will cover it) into sort of android robots or avatars. This will be done by some mysterious process in which the human's persona is loaded electronically into a robot, rendering that human immortal, or at least able to exist until the robots get in a fight and destroy one another, or until an asteroid crashes into the earth and does away with the whole kit and caboodle. Mr. Itskov is appealing to over a thousand other billionaires to join him in funding the program. Not only will they all be made immortal, so the sales pitch goes, but they will make a whole bunch of money in the humanoid robot business. With this appeal, the billionaires make economics a cohort of religion and science in the search for immortality.

Health magazines don't exactly promise everlasting life, but they don't exactly *not* promise it, either. Behind their helpful, prescriptive instructions, and especially their photographs, is the promise that you can stay forever young. All you have to do is exercise, eat properly, and buy the products the magazines advertise. The sign of holiness, if you do so, is not a halo over the head, but a flat belly and skin that never wrinkles. Various foods, medicines, and diet supplements ensure enduring youth à la Ponce de León's fabled fountain. The irony of the situation is how many people, given the choice of eternal youth or gluttony, choose the latter. If any of this healthy hopefulness really delivered, there would be quite a few people over a hundred years old still playing soccer.

But who am I to make fun of these keys to everlasting life? Maybe one of them will actually work. However, figuring out where we would put all those immortal people is another thing. What would we do with a population of hundreds of billions when we don't have resources to keep seven billion from killing one another over the remaining supply of land and fuel?

The theologians and scientists have thought about that. For theologians, the solution is easier, requiring only fervent ideology to seemingly make it happen. Happy hunting grounds of the spirit do not require space since spiritualized bodies don't occupy space. How convenient. For the scientific mind, colonizing material happy hunting grounds requires a somewhat bigger challenge to one's faith. One must, again, drum up some kind of material infinitude. One must consider that the number of planets out there ready and waiting to house an infinite number of people is unlimited.

Whether steeped in science or in religion, the human mind in the face of immortality and infinity starts thinking in similar ways. Both must have faith that somewhere in outer or inner "space," the solution to our fear of death and mortality lies waiting for us. Atheists might scoff at the idea of resting forever in the arms of Jesus, but is that notion any sillier than trying to find another earth to live on, a one-in-an-infinity shot surely? Nor would that solve the problem, because we would have to kill off the inhabitants of such a newly discovered planet like we killed off the Native Americans. Looking for eternity would be like voting for one of two great scams: the infallible space program or the infallible Vatican. And what if the people of the new earth were farther advanced than us technologically or had a more powerful god? Who would kill off whom? And if we won, would we be happy with the kind of immortality that the Space Age suggests: a constant war with other planets?

The scientific keys to everlasting life are as flawed as the theological keys, but I wonder if maybe the latter are not cleverer. All you have to do in theological belief systems is obey the word of the God of your choice. If you screw up occasionally, you can be forgiven. Prostitutes of the sexual or the money kind can become preachers of virtue in their old age, and quite often they do. However, with scientific screwups, for instance nuclear bombs, second chances might not be possible. Praying your way to immortality is certainly more economical and ecological than, say, freezing and storing bodies for the scientific day of resurrection. When you read the fine print behind the theological guarantees of eternal life, you realize that you are expected to pay your way of course, but contributing to the wealth of the clergy is such a paltry sum compared with building rockets to take you to some pie in the sky beyond the Phoenix Cluster.

Why isn't it so much simpler and more reasonable to find immortality and infinity in the eternal garden, in the ever-renewing food chain? I should be able to answer that question myself. I had believed that I would die and go to heaven if I behaved myself. Discarding that notion, but still imbued with the idea that there had to be something out there someplace to make me immortal, I convinced myself that advances in science really could bring everlasting physical life someday (although, being of a practical turn of mind, I was willing to settle for a couple hundred years). I believed in the first kind of nonsense because my parents, grandparents, and early teachers believed it. I loved them and they loved me. They were good people and we all shared a good life. Why would I not believe them? The error of enlightened disbelievers is to think that all of us who depart the believing life do so with a spirit of joy and relief at finally having escaped intellectual blindness. That was not true for me. I loved my happy Catholic world despite the absurdity of some of its dogma. I loved the idea of living forever in a happy hunting ground, especially since I loved to hunt rabbits and squirrels. So when the logic of new knowledge forced me to disbelief, I carried on awhile in the old way because I did not want to hurt my parents' feelings, did not want to alienate myself from family and friends. Loyalty can easily become a curse. And besides, theological matters were not really that important to me. When I knelt piously in church, I was really meditating on complicated football plays sure to produce touchdowns.

In my new religion based on "reason," I merely transferred the theological way of thinking to science. I used the same thought parameters, the same methodology of picking and choosing major premises that seemed to apply and tossing out the others. Then I began to see that scientists were not always pursuing truth, either, but rather the money that the wealthy and powerful would pay them to champion their favorite major premises, just like religion did. I became a maverick, suspicious of both religion and science. But I kept my doubts to myself. It was bad enough incurring the wrath of religious ideologues; if I wrote that science seemed prone to ideology, too, I would be shunned by both sides. I had seen journalists lose jobs and assignments for their anti-religious or anti-science opinions. I kept silent and looked for little havens of integrity in both religion and science that did not offend anyone too much. Or I wrote humor. My boss at *Farm Journal* magazine was so afraid that farm advertisers might think my columns were undermining the religion and science of agribusiness, and that farmers might start to take them seriously, that he had the layout artists slug them with a big, bold heading: HUMOR. Just so there was no confusion.

My reward for being a maverick led me toward a kind of aloof intellectual aloneness that, among other things, inexplicably lessened my fear of death. I even began to see some advantages in death. No more listening to news reports that quoted ultra-right-wing talk show primitives, for example. This new peace, which was oozing up out of my joy in having my own little farm (my heavenly kingdom), took me one step further toward coming to terms with the dichotomy between religion and science. I began to feel sorry for the victims of both. The fear of death was so embedded in the human psyche that no attempt to overcome it by either prayer or scientific experiment, however pathetic, should be ridiculed, I decided. Any ideology that softened the sorrow of death was okay, so long as it did not lead to cruelty and injustice. Even right-wing talk show primitives had their moments.

Think of that real raw moment of a child watching his mother die. What *should* you say to him? Is ideology one way or another going to make much difference?

Perhaps education should be teaching another way out of the dilemma, another way to come to terms with reality. What if we, as loving parents and conscientious teachers, told children that, yes, someday, the people you love are going to die but they will always live in your memory safe from both the strife and suffering of life and the inscrutable agony of spiritual immortality. Our bodies are made of chemicals and organic matter that do not go to any paradise up in the sky somewhere but into a peaceful slumber of humus in old Mother Earth where, in one form or another, they live forever. If that were taught universally, is it possible that everyone would be happier, accepting the idea that in mortality lies immortality?

But I did not say any of this out loud for a long time. I did not want to be considered an outcast. I just laid low on my little farm and made my own paradise.

CHAPTER 7

--------- ◆ ---------

Georgie the Cat

*G*eorgie was just a plain old everyday cat. But to Jerry, our four-year-old son, she was his first experience in friendship outside our circle of family love. Georgie brought him mice; he gave Georgie cookies. When Jerry shrank back in fear, Georgie faced off the raccoon that in Jerry's eyes had come on the patio to eat the kittens. Georgie and Jerry had shared emotions, had, in a four-year-old boy's world, ridden the river together.

And now Jerry had found his cat lying dead inside the barn door. He came to me with dread stamped on his face. He had seen death but did not know what death was.

"Daddy. Daddy. Georgie." That is all he could say. Afraid to say more, perhaps, afraid that his words would make it real.

I found the shovel, slid it under Georgie, and lifted her. And right then Jerry knew death for sure because Georgie would never have allowed herself to be picked up on the end of any shovel on earth.

Tears streaked down his chin, but I had nerve for only one look into eyes that were second by second learning about a world that ends all living with dying. I turned my back, walked resolutely toward the woods, my shovel heavy beyond all rational explanation. And Jerry came along, though every whimper and wail protested.

Even as he cried, he began to ask questions, and he asked all the right ones, all the unanswered pleas of all humans in the face of death. And I had to answer.

"Can she see us yet, Daddy? Does she know she's on that shovel?"

I did not say what I wanted to say. I did not tell him that Georgie was up in some cat heaven, smiling down on us from a misty world where the mice were plump and the milk thick with cream.

"No, Jerry, Georgie can't see us anymore."

"Can't she even feel? Can't she move at all?"

"No, she can't move or feel."

"Make her move." Jerry grabbed me around my leg, begged me, the man who, in his eyes, could do anything in the world.

"I can't, Jerry. When something is dead, you can't do anything about it." I laid down the shovel, and held his head against me and knew I wasn't going to be able to take it much longer.

"We must bury Georgie," I finally said and started resolutely toward the woods again.

"What is bury?"

"We will dig a hole and put Georgie in it and cover her up," I said.

"Why?"

We were almost to the woods and I did not have the slightest idea why we had to cover Georgie up with dirt.

"That is what you do when something dies."

"Can I touch her, Daddy? Does she feel like she did before?"

"Yes, you may touch her if you want, but she won't feel you."

The boy stooped and petted his dead cat. He became the scientist now, moving from the fear of primitive man in the face of death to the dawn of scientific curiosity. He was trying to diagnose death with his hands and I could not endure it.

"We will put Georgie in the ground so nothing can disturb her," I said.

"Will you put a fence around so nobody can step on her?" he asked. I think I know how cemeteries got started.

"Put a rock on her so we always know where she's at," he said. I could not believe my ears. He didn't know about tombstones but his mind was surely the mind of all mankind.

"Yes, that's a good idea. Go by the barn there and get one of those rocks to put on top." It gave him something to do while I shoveled dirt.

But the hole was not wide enough and he was back again before I got the crude rites of burial over with. Then as I started to push the dirt in, he began to cry again and I had no more strength left in me. We wept together. I wondered why, in an odd sort of way, I could weep now over a mere cat more than I had wept over my mother's burial. But my hand was around my son and I was weeping for him more than for the cat. Or maybe it was because I did not have to push the dirt in on Mother's grave.

"Won't she ever, ever, ever get back up?" Jerry bawled, begging for immortality, the poor bleating cry of all humans in all times. And I could only shake my head.

"If the old cats don't die, there would no room for the young ones. If our old hens didn't die, where would we put the pullets?"

I don't know whether he understood, or whether I did, but that is what I said because I didn't know what else to say. We filled in the dirt and went away. Jerry now knew something more about death; I knew something more about life.

But that was not quite the end of it. Jerry appeared to dismiss Georgie from consciousness. But he spent much more time with his kitten, Georgie's last gift to him. For two days the kitten wouldn't eat, and Carol and I worried. If the kitten died . . . was it too much to ask of a boy four going on five? We spent a lot of time trying to make the kitten drink milk, displaying a cheery airiness, as if to show Jerry there was nothing more normal than a kitten that didn't eat for two days. But Jerry was not fooled.

On the third day, I was up at the barn with the chickens and I heard a whoop of joy. Jerry was running up the path to me, his kitten in his arm.

"Daddy, Daddy, Frisky drank his milk. He's going to be all right now, Mommy says. He's going to *live!*" And the bright boy eyes shone up at me with all the hope that has kept mankind going for who knows how many millions of years. And I think Jerry learned more than he realized. Now he sees that Georgie is dead, but Frisky lives.

Someday, I will die but his children will live. And then he will understand how I feel now: Mother is gone but Jerry lives, *and so then does she.*

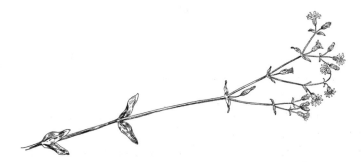

CHAPTER 8

Intimations of Immortality I: The Chickweed Version

I don't want to call chickweed the worst weed in the garden because I think it is trying to teach us a lesson about everlasting life. In its preferred field of operation—that is, rich organic soil—chickweed is almost indestructible. Oh, you can blot it out with a thick layer of mulch. That will last for almost a whole growing season, which for chickweed is the whole year. Look out, though, when the mulch decays away. The green terror comes roaring back.

A year like 2012 seems to tell us that chickweed will be with us always. The winter never got really cold where I live. Chickweed, which can grow when the temperature gets above about fifty degrees Fahrenheit, never really quits growing completely, even in January. In all the garden plots where I thought I had won some control over it, the nasty stuff spread like the plague during winter thaws. By the end of February it was ready to go to seed, guaranteeing another century of existence.

Then March came and with it weather that we usually get in May. The ground was soaked; the air was warm. Chickweed switched into super-NASCAR growth speed. By the time the ground was dry enough to cultivate, it had transformed itself into a mat four inches thick and of course was blooming. Have you ever tried to take on a carpet of four-inch thickness with a garden tiller? The tiller just bounced off that stuff like a child on a trampoline. So I sharpened my hoe to a razor's edge and attacked. Chop. Bounce. Chop. Bounce. Chop. Bounce. I might as well have tried to hoe a mattress. In fury, I knelt down and started ripping the green hellion out of the ground with my bare hands. Where it was really rooted down, I didn't have the strength to pull it out. Where I could get it loose, it came up in great gobs that removed two inches of topsoil with it. I finally got out my big field disk and tractor and ripped through the mat. Then the garden tiller would, in three or four passes, work the stuff into big brown clods that I could remove by hand or manure fork.

Chemical weed killers will turn the green mattress into a yellow one. The yellow, half-dead growth is just as hard to till through. And soon, oh so very soon, new green troops arrive at the scene. I decided I was dealing with a form of eternal life, another version of my bewilderment about life everlasting.

I've never tried it myself, but other gardeners tell me that the best way to snuff out chickweed's quest for immortality is with a flamethrower. They say it is worth the money to buy one of those gas weed flamers just for the orgasmic satisfaction one gets while scorching the living hell out of the weed. But the flamer doesn't kill the tangle of roots and infinite number of seeds underground. Let's say you plant corn following your scorched-earth policy. By August, if it rains more than three drops, a million new chickweed seedlings explode under the tall corn. It is kind of hard to maneuver a flamethrower in that situation unless you want a lot of roasting ears or popcorn all at once.

Chickens and livestock will eat chickweed sure enough. If you pen a flock of hens on a garden plot, as with a movable "chicken tractor," you will be rid of the chickweed, but only for awhile unless you've discovered chickweed's Achilles' heel, which is not to cultivate at all. Chickweed won't compete with *permanent* pasture grasses. It won't persist in a lawn, either. Its environment is regularly cultivated soil. The more you grind at it with a tiller, the better it grows. And that's the lesson it is trying to teach us, I think. Chickweed is nature's way of reminding us that annual soil tillage is unnatural and unsustainable—unless you want to live on chickweed salad, which by the way is not bad.

At the same time that I was locked in mortal combat with chickweed I was experimenting with rotational grazing as a form of "permanent" farming, notwithstanding the fact that wherever enough rain falls to grow trees, forestland is the "permanent" natural situation, the so-called climax vegetation. Farm animals by nature get their food by grazing. The new agricultural wisdom maintained that if nutritional grasses and clovers were available, livestock and chickens would produce meat, milk, and eggs just as well, and much more economically, than being penned up and stuffed with annual grains. So I decided to give it a try. I divided my little acreage into eight plots of about an acre each, and had at it. It was not as easy as I thought it would be—in fact, good pasture farming requires lots of management. But it did work if I mowed regularly to control thorny trees and bushes. The success of the system, I learned, was to rotate the animals from one plot to another in a way that encourages the pasture plants to regrow vigorously when not being grazed, thus providing fresh, lush grazing throughout the growing season. Managing rotations so that the animals do not return to the same plot more than once every six weeks helps greatly to control internal parasites in the animals, too.

My dream, following all the gurus of pasture farming, was to raise meat, milk, and eggs without ever having to cultivate the soil. To my surprise, a ton of books (almost literally) proclaimed the advantages of permanent pastures. The animals' droppings plus the additions of plant food, especially nitrogen, from the legumes provide all the fertilizer needed. Judicious mowing at the end of the grazing cycle in each plot, or for hay, plus the grazing itself, controls most unwanted weeds. The savings in time, machinery, and fuel by not tearing up the soil with monster machines every year were monumental. Soil erosion is reduced to almost nothing. The high concentration of roots in pasture soils means a much higher number and variety of beneficial microorganisms live there, not to mention beneficial insects like earthworms. Pastures build humus, the lifeblood of the food chain. And permanent pasture is one of the most effective ways to sequester carbon. Some advocates of pasture farming go so far as to say that disturbing the soil even once by cultivation destroys the natural balance of soil life that only a century of permanent pasture can restore.

Imagine an American rural landscape that looks like a golf course rather than amber waves of grain from sea to shining sea. As a matter of fact, in some places in Europe there actually are golf courses being pastured, as was true of the sport's beginning years in Scotland. If pasture farming works, it means transforming the earth into a perpetual garden of paradise, especially if golf is your favorite pastime.

The longer the animals graze in winter, the less hay has to be made, and so the search continues for plants that provide grazing even when snow covers the ground. (The buffalo managed to live for eons pawing the dry, dead, but still nutritional grass out of the snow.) Some native prairie grasses and some fescues work fairly well to add another month or two of winter grazing, even in the North. Clovers die in cold weather, but the dead forage still makes good grazing until snow flattens it.

Surveying all the possibilities made me think of chickweed. Aha. Maybe it was the ideal winter grazing plant. It regenerates itself only too well and is succulent enough to be eaten by livestock and chickens. Even here in northern Ohio it stays green into December, and starts growing again in March or, as I learned in 2012, even in February. If climate change so dictates, maybe it will grow all winter long. Greatly excited, I tried to get chickweed started in my pastures. To my chagrin, it wouldn't cooperate. It would not grow in undisturbed soil. It was intimating its own version of immortality versus mortality right there in the grass. If you want a truly sustainable kind of farming, don't tear up the soil with constant cultivation, it seemed to say. If you do, then you have to deal with things like chickweed, not to mention thorns and thistles and poison ivy and ragweed and other plants that also proliferate on disturbed soil. Or to quote the King James version of the Bible where God drives Adam and Eve from their garden of paradise: ". . . cursed is the ground for thy sake; in sorrow thou shalt eat of it all the days of thy life. Thorns also and thistles shall it bring forth to thee and thou shalt eat the herb of the field." Like so many passages in the Bible, I'm not quite sure what that means, so I feel free to interpret this one differently from the way the theologians generally do. Perhaps the forbidden fruit of any real garden of paradise is any food from annually cultivated soil. Maybe chickweed is trying to tell us that ripping up soil every year is the first step away from the eternal garden that the earth could be.

In the meantime, some intrepid souls make and sell a chickweed healing salve that they say is effective against rashes, chapped skin, and skin abrasions of various kinds. Maybe if I smeared enough on me, I would live forever.

CHAPTER 9

Intimations
of Immortality II:
The Pigweed Version

*T*he biggest immediate threat to farming in the second decade of the twenty-first century appears not to be recession, climate change, Monsanto, creeping social-ism, or primitive Evangelicalism, but a plant with the racy name of pigweed. It is also called, in barnyard Ohio lingo, redroot because of its pinkish root. More properly it is amaranth, which actually does sound a little racy. If you want to be really highbrow, call it *Amaranthus retroflexus* or *A. hybridus* and then sort of look wisely off toward the horizon as if everyone knew that. If you want to sound really up to the minute, call it Palmer amaranth because that's the particular kind, out of about sixty named species, that is giving the herbicide industry fits. Weed scientists are calling Palmer amaranth "the perfect weed" (as in "the perfect storm") or

Superweed because it has become immune to glyphosate herbicides. It certainly is the plant to study for those seeking ways to attain immortality. At a Bayer CropScience experimental plot in Illinois recently, it had "completely overrun the soybeans in most of the plots" despite having had nearly everything in the present weed-killing arsenal thrown at it.

This is bad news for grain farmers, who can only hope that "science" soon comes up with an herbicide strong enough to kill the stuff without turning the landscape into a barren desert. So I must sound like an agricultural anarchist when I suggest that Palmer amaranth might someday be our ally, not our enemy. It thrives in dry hot weather (most pigweeds do) because it was originally a southwestern desert plant that migrated across the South and now is marching resolutely into the Midwest. It is a good answer to the kind of drought we experienced in 2012. It also fixes carbon very efficiently and can grow one to two inches a day, which in my observation is true of the native pigweeds that love to pop up in my garden in July, no matter how dry it is.

But here's the irony. Pigweed grain, even Palmer amaranth grain, has been recognized as a nutritious food for something like eight thousand years. It was a staple for the Aztecs and even the North American mound-building Indians. More than likely it was grown by the Woodland Indians who erected the mound along Warpole Creek. It is still eaten all over Mexico, especially as a popped grain mixed in with honey to make a candy called *alegria*. Bob Rodale made amaranth a major endeavor at the Rodale Institute's farm in eastern Pennsylvania starting back in the 1970s. The institute developed new strains of the weed, devoted acres to growing them, started a seed bank for them, and spread the word worldwide about the weed's potential to replace other grains in many instances. Bob, with whom I was closely associated at the time, was convinced that he was on to a major new crop, a commercial grain that could yield as well as maize or rice in many situations, especially where dry weather is a factor.

The situation was a little embarrassing for me. I was doing a lot of writing for Rodale Press at the time and was very much impressed with the possibilities of amaranth, and even more impressed with Bob Rodale's innovative genius. But the first time I saw a whole field of pigweed in orderly rows, I had a feeling that I was staring into something akin to a field version of Soylent Green. As I child on the farm and in the garden, I had been taught that pigweed was evil, something to be exterminated even, which never happened. You let one pigweed go to seed and next year you have to deal with a hundred million of the infernal devils. Wrenching loose the roots of my cultural upbringing even more, there was also a whole field of lamb's-quarter on the farm in neat, otherwise weedless rows. Lamb's-quarter (*Chenopodium album*) is another good human food, prized in places like India, but hated in the kind of farming into which I was born. I looked sideways at Bob, standing next to me, not daring to face him directly. "Do you realize what you are doing to me?" I asked him. "This is like show-ing a fervent Christian that hell is a really nice place to live." He just smiled that huge, mysterious smile of his, taking my comment as a compliment, as indeed I had meant it to be.

For awhile, we all thought that, in the future, amaranth would be right up there with corn and sow bellies on the commodities exchange at the Chicago Board of Trade. Everything pointed toward that kind of future, and even commercial farmers in Illinois were doing large field plantings of the "new" grain. I visited and wrote about farmers and gardeners who were as excited about pigweed as they were about soybeans. Soybeans have more protein content—30 to 40 percent—compared with 14 to 18 percent for grain amaranth, but the latter has a more complete protein than any common grain or legume. Everything pointed to a great future for amaranth.

But strangely, I could never bring myself to plant any in my own garden. Every time I looked at the little sack of seed I had brought home from the Rodale Farm with me, I was filled with shame. All I could see in my mind's eye were legions of pigweed spreading like kudzu, another good intention gone awry, across the farmlands of America. I just couldn't plant any. Eventually, feeling like a traitor, I burned the seed in a bonfire. Acculturation once more triumphed over intellectualization.

As it turned out, that's what happened throughout the farming society, too, as far as my knowledge extends. Grain amaranth never caught on very well. The main reason was that the seeds are so tiny and the plants grow quite tall and ungainly, seven or eight feet anyway. Machine harvesting and handling are exceedingly difficult on a large scale and very tedious on a small scale. The Aztecs, after all, did not live in a piston-driven society. Preindustrial civilizations were content to gather grain amaranth slowly and painstakingly from the wild because that's what they did. The only kind of horticulture or agriculture comparable to it today in terms of hand planting and harvesting is marijuana. We will work that hard for a drug because right now that is the only way to get it. We won't do it for food because we don't have to. Not so many years ago, seed catalogs like Johnny's Selected Seeds, which I think was the first to do so, carried grain amaranth. Now Johnny's and most other companies sell it only as an ornamental plant, and it is indeed beautiful. Seeds of Change (and I'm sure a few other catalogs) still sells grain amaranth, but there is not the emphasis on it as formerly. Hardly anyone is still pointing out that the seeds have a balance of proteins and amino acids that in some ways is equivalent to beef and just maybe better than beef for human nutrition.

So now we have a dilemma, which I should not joke about, I guess, but I can't help it. We have a wild plant that threatens our commercial grain industry because it likes a swig of herbicide occasionally. Amaranth is a key in the search for the eternal garden. It just might outlive Monsanto. Not only has it endured for unnumbered centuries, but it is now on the counterattack. If it could talk it would release a news bulletin saying that since humans have rejected it as a commercial food, it will do its best to change our minds and force its natural and pragmatic philosophy of life upon us. It is marching into our industrial grain fields, hoping to save us from ourselves and persuade us to abandon our piston-engined food production system for the old hoe.

Actually the hoe won't really be the only or best way to work with amaranth to make a more immortal world for humans. For example, hogs love the pinkish roots of the plant, which I presume is how the plant got the name pigweed. We could graze pork on more or less permanent, self-renewing fields of amaranth much more economically than harvesting corn and hauling it to pig factories. The young leaves of amaranth are good in salads, too, for humans as well as pigs. And the seeds that the pigs don't eat can be used in all kinds of protein-rich baked goods. When a drought year like 2012 comes along, the amaranth garden farmer (the only kind left if we survive a couple more centuries) can yawn and go fishing. Well, on second thought, since amaranth still grows vigorously in dry weather, we'll still have to hoe where we don't want the stuff.

And by the way, when the Rodale folks started growing pigweed and lamb's-quarter in a somewhat artificial, industrial way—that is, in large plantings where other plants were excluded—these wild foods started having disease and fertility problems, just like commercial grains. In terms of achieving immortality, there must be a lesson here. We all know what it is. Large, industrial monocropping just ain't natural. Large, concentrated populations of people in large cities who need large, industrial monocropping to stay alive ain't natural, either.

CHAPTER 10

Why Are They
Killing Themselves?

*W*hile I was trying to understand the difference between mortality and immortality, suicide was poking its ugly head prominently into the news. Suicides in the military jumped 15 percent in 2012. (So the headlines said. I no longer believe anybody's numbers for sure.) Teenage suicides were occurring with mystifying frequency, and the second leading cause of death among college students was suicide, again, so the headlines said. In my own little world, an Amish farmer, the last sort of person I would have believed suicidal, killed himself in his barn. So did a young woman I knew who had everything going for her. The fact of these deaths coupled with my own overwhelming desire to live forever collided in my brain with such force that for a time I could not handle both realities at the same time. Why do people kill themselves? If we have advanced so much in health care, why can't we slow down the suicide rate? Why do people who in outward appearance seem to have a good life kill themselves while sad sacks with seemingly nothing to live for go on bitching about life well into their nineties? Why do people with all kinds of problems not kill themselves more often? That awful word: Why? Why is the name of the witch that rides on our backs, clawing at us, shrieking into our ears, taunting us because we will not admit what she knows: There are never enough answers to satisfy our eternal quest for them.

I studied the statistics on suicide. Or tried to. As is so often the case in the hunt for facts, the numbers about suicide, and the information on what causes it, are ambiguous and ambivalent. In the first place, suicides are sometimes reported as "accidents" to save the family from more anguish. Second, it is not always known when accidents are really suicides. Furthermore, we live now in a society where assisted suicide is a crime, so no one knows how many deaths from "accidental overdose" or from so-called natural causes are actually assisted suicides. Hospice workers tell me about patients full of pain and misery, with no hope at all of recovering, with death only days away, begging their caretakers to smother them with their pillows. Others starve themselves to death. The real crime here is the law against assisted suicides.

Once you get past all the caveats, information about suicide is still suspect. Dentists do not commit suicide more than any other professional people, although physicians and health workers in general are high on some lists. People with a history of mental illness do not kill themselves any more than others not thought to have serious mental illness. Suicides do not increase in the Thanksgiving/Christmas/New Year's holiday season. The numbers more often seem to rise in the spring, the season, supposedly, of renewed hope. More men than women kill themselves, but women just as often try to kill themselves and fail. Maybe they are just faking it. Maybe they change their minds at the last second. If all those interminable numbers I find on Google are correct, suicide rates in general have risen slightly since around 2000, but are no higher now than in 1950. This did not surprise me, because of what I had learned by accident about the late 1800s and early 1900s. Doing research on an entirely different subject, I had to read many editions of our local papers on microfilm. To my surprise, more suicides were reported back then than now.

The very latest data to come out in 2013 says that suicides among the middle-aged are up. When you look at the fine print, though, there are so many "yes, buts" that the statistics seem less than compelling. The numbers have something to do with the Baby Boomer spike in population now going into middle age. But why should the most spoiled generation in our history be committing suicide more often than other age groups?

The problem is made only more confusing by cultural attitudes. So deeply implanted into our minds is the idea that suicide is immoral that any discussion about what to do about it lapses into emotional debate involving ideologies. Not even something seemingly so easy to count as the number of suicides in the military today will go unchallenged. Anti-war advocates have their numbers and pro-war advocates hasten to counter with the question of how many of those would have committed suicide if they had not been in the military. And no one knows how many battlefield deaths are in fact suicides.

In case histories of suicides I have studied, neither science nor religion seemed to be a major influence. Atheists don't kill themselves any more often than churchgoers. Some people who admit to suicidal tendencies tell me that they have found mental health professionals full of fancy words that on close examination are empty of real meaning. Others make the same exact criticism of religious efforts to help them. One such complained to me that listening to a preacher talking piously about living forever "bathed in the glow of God's everlasting light" was so depressing to him that it drove him to more thoughts of suicide.

Nor do the statistics indicate conclusively whether genetic causes are to blame. Sometimes suicide does seem to run in families, but that, too, depends on definition. If a great-aunt kills herself and then her great-niece does the same, is that running in families? Many people are now being helped out of clinical depression with various medications, but there is no sure evidence that clinically depressed people commit suicide any more than other groups. Neither alcoholism nor drug addiction necessarily leads to suicide. If either did, we would be losing population dramatically. Are there maybe wayward genes in the suicide's DNA that are the culprit? Undetected tumors in the brain? Some connection of nerve and synapse gone awry? Science can't say conclusively. Does mental or sexual abuse in childhood bring on suicide? Maybe, but most sexually or mentally abused people do not commit suicide.

It is popular to blame suicide on increasing social pressure to perform better. The statistics do not seem to support that, either. Some say youthful suicide comes from pushing children too much in school and sports. But most children stressed that way not only do not commit suicide, but seem to thrive under the pressure. All things considered, children surely have it much better today than in earlier societies where they slaved away in dirty factories without the protection of child labor laws. Most of them, obviously, did not commit suicide. Women, too, are expected to perform superhumanly well as mothers at home and workers outside the homes, and that situation is sometimes blamed for depression that leads to suicide. But again, most women endure this challenge amazingly well. I doubt if the millennial generation is anywhere near as bad off as those women of yesteryear, living raw, unrelenting lives of austerity and hardship, exposed to wildlife and Indian attacks, without electricity or proper health care. I know what it is like to live in a ramshackle farmhouse without electricity. I watched my mother as she stood in that desolate kitchen the day we moved in and wept. But she soon got over it. She made that house into a wonderful family gathering place. I remember her almost always singing as she went about her servile work. One of my fond memories is how she would heat up a sad iron, wrap it in a towel, and put it at the foot of my bed to keep my feet warm on cold nights. That was luxury, not hardship.

Obviously, I was not doing this examination and cross-examination of suicide just out of idle curiosity. Facing old age and feeling that there was something wrong with the way my body was acting, thoughts of death kept pushing into my consciousness. I knew I could never just outright kill myself no matter what. But because I had a strong distaste of being in public places, especially hospitals, I wondered if, in serious sickness in old age, I would have the guts to just stay at home and let death come with a lot of help from morphine—a passive form of suicide. Eerily, moralists seem to have fewer qualms over passive suicide. But whenever I mentioned anything to that effect around family members, they gave every indication that they would never allow me to be that stupid. It dawned on me slowly that this dying business was not really as much my decision as I had thought it was supposed to be. The last duty of a good father and husband was to somehow make life easier for the surviving family, even to the bitter end. Well, maybe. But I started to make a point of bringing the subject of my death up casually in conversation, sort of to get people, including myself, used to it.

Trying to make up for my own smattering of knowledge about how psychiatry and psychology handle suicidal tendencies, I found a couple of people who suffered severe clinical depression and who were willing to talk about their state of mind. They absolutely insisted that their condition came from a chemical imbalance in their systems that only certain combinations of medical chemicals had been able to control. They described their depression as extreme mental anguish and physical pain that only those who suffer it can understand or appreciate. No amount of psychiatric advice or group therapy was of any help to them, they said. They got relief from their pills, but successful medication depended upon a practitioner who was willing and able to continually vary the amounts of the medicine until just the right combinations brought relief.

They directed me to read David Foster Wallace, the writer who eventually committed suicide himself. Here's a quote from Wallace you can find on the Internet: "The so-called psychotically depressed person who tries to kill herself doesn't do so out of quote 'hopelessness' or an abstract conviction that life's assets and debits do not square. And surely not because death seems suddenly appealing. The person in whom its [depression's] invisible agony reaches a certain unendurable level will kill herself in the same way a trapped person will eventually jump from a window of a burning high rise. . . ." The unthinkable crept into my mind. What if, for these people, assisted suicide might be as proper as I think it should be for those with serious incurable disease who know they will die soon and who have nothing but pain and misery to look forward to until then?

But who can say? The human mind is so devious and complicated, I wondered if I could believe my informants completely. They surely thought they were telling the truth, but because most clinically depressed people do not commit suicide, including my informants, how could I be sure of what they were saying about suicide? And regardless, many people commit suicide who are not diagnosed with severe clinical depression. How should they be judged?

Let us say, for sake of mind-stretching, that suicide is not that simple or complicated. Let us suppose that in many cases we are looking for its root causes in the wrong way or the wrong place. People who commit suicide almost always are remembered for having expressed negative opinions of their own worth during their lifetimes. My informants flatly insisted that their affliction had nothing to do with their attitude toward themselves or their environment. But since they did not in fact commit suicide, at least not yet, might I suggest other possibilities about those who do? Many of them were in the habit of speaking deprecatingly of themselves. How much of that feeling of worthlessness do we teach unintentionally through cultural attitudes?

A most penetrating essay on suicide appeared in *The New Yorker* of March 11, 2013, "Requiem for a Dream" by Larissa MacFarquhar. It examines the possible reasons why the computer genius Aaron Swartz took his life recently at the age of twenty-six after being indicted on multiple felony counts for downloading material on the Internet in a way that was considered to be illegal. Swartz was already highly successful and faced a future of even more promise, even if he would have had to spend a short time in jail. In this account, his friends and family weighed in on their views of why he had killed himself and I read avidly, hoping for revelation. But even these close and intimate views offered no satisfying answer to the Why Witch. Swartz's father concluded the article by saying: "You know, it just doesn't seem to make sense to me . . . I just think it's a question I'll never answer."

But something Swartz revealed about himself bore down on my mind. Long before he committed suicide, MacFarquhar quotes Aaron as saying: "I feel my existence is an imposition on the planet." How did he come to such a ridiculous conclusion? I advance an answer hesitantly, knowing full well that I will be challenged. But for a moment, try to step completely outside the cultural cocoon from which almost all of us have emerged. If we could from childhood be taught that we are such an integral part of life that we flow from the food chain and will be enfolded back into it, and that there is a comforting beauty in that realization far more satisfying than spending eternity in communion with some mysterious godly presence, could anyone ever think of himself or herself as an imposition on the planet? That kind of talk comes from a centuries-old philosophical idealism that has succeeded in convincing us that we are god-like spirits apart from the planet and destined for a kind of spiritual afterlife that in reality does not exist.

I think of Francis of Assisi, once a kind of hero to me (in some ways he still is). He was quite the wild one before he gave up the vanities of wealth and turned to a life of poverty. He also embraced a close relationship to nature on his way to becoming a revered saint of the Catholic Church. If there had been psychiatrists around in his day like we have today, however, I'm sure his mental health report card would have very few A's on it during the years that he struggled to find his place in life. In his moments of despondency, he likened himself to a lowly worm. He said a regular prayer in which he repeated that lowly worm metaphor. As a Franciscan seminarian studying for the priesthood, I was taught that this prayer showed admirable humility. But surely this was not a way to boost a person's attitude about himself.

Unless. Let us look at this from an entirely different perspective. If a person were brought up in a culture where natural human proclivities were not thought to be sinful or dirty, that far from being lowly, worms were very highly beneficial forms of life—which of course they are—would such a conviction reduce the despondency and depression humans often feel? Could it even reduce the suicide rate? No more would be heard that old folkloric doggerel:

> *Nobody loves me; everybody hates me.*
> *I'm goin' down and dig worms.*
> *Big ones, little ones,*
> *Fat ones, skinny ones,*
> *I'm goin' down and dig worms.*

In an enlightened culture, the ditty would go like this:

> *Everybody loves me, nobody hates me,*
> *I'm gonna dance with the worms.*
> *Sleek ones, shiny ones,*
> *Gorgeous ones, lovely ones,*
> *I'm gonna dance with the worms.*

Francis in his old age began to use the words *Brother Death* when referring to his demise. Surely that is evidence that he had found a way to accept the inevitable in a mentally healthful way. No wonder legend says that the wild birds flocked around him. I would not be too surprised if that were true. Many of us who embrace nature know the pleasure of having chickadees and nuthatches flock around us as we reload our bird feeders. Not in our lowest moments would we ever say that our existence is an imposition on the planet. We know we are an inseparable part of all life.

When weighed down with disappointment over failure in some particular endeavor, or with loathing for the idiocies of the human race (including my own), or simply over the passing of time and the inevitably of death, I find that such despondency disappears when I am working in the garden or in the woods, or listening to music I love, especially natural music. I wonder if it would help suicidal people to spend lots of time in the garden, doing the meaningful work of producing food in partnership with nature and surrounded by wood thrush, meadowlark, and song sparrow, all of them singing away. In the garden, the Why Witch disappears from my consciousness. I no longer ask stupid questions for which there are no answers. Might that also be the case with the suicidal?

But I can hear immediately an objection. Maybe making death more comforting would only encourage people to kill themselves more often. First of all, that is extremely unlikely. If it were not, many more Christians and Muslims would become suicide bombers in defense of their religion because they firmly believe they will go straight to their heaven if they die defending their faith. As a matter of fact, people who think they are headed for an eternity of bliss fight just as hard to stay alive as anyone else. What I think would rather happen, if death were accepted as the natural ending of life, is that suicide would be decriminalized and that would in itself lower the suicide rate. Just as death cafés are becoming popular, I see in a more enlightened future what will be called death parties (though let's give them a less repugnant name, like *final farewell parties*), where, instead of being an awful, evil, barbaric practice, suicide would become a sort of sacrament. The person wishing to reenter the food chain, having exhausted all efforts to stay alive in any kind of fulfilling way, and with death imminent, would be allowed to gather with friends and family and, after suitable celebration, take the pills or whatever that would end life painlessly.

As objectionable as that sounds to our culture, this idea is being discussed in death cafés and around kitchen tables where the iron grip of religious tradition no longer holds sway. I am convinced that in this situation, many potential suicide victims would change their minds. But if they did go ahead, surrounded by loving friends and family, surely that is better than sneaking off into the barn and hanging themselves with the hay rope or going into the woods alone and blowing their heads off with a shotgun.

I humor myself into thinking that if we were brought up appreciating how natural ways toward contentment are so much more effective than supernatural ways, that in fact supernatural ways exist only in human minds, we just might be comforted enough in the face of life's adversities to seek solace in meaningful work away from the world's strife, bringing on a kind of tranquility where the idea of deliberate self-destruction would rarely present itself. It is presumptuous of me, but I am convinced that if all of us, from childhood on, were taught that real life after death is right here in the real world, we might find solace and peace enough in the living NOW to satisfy our restless souls. We might even start thinking more about the possibility of true peace coming into the world if all of us understood that right here on earth is where the only possible sources of true contentment lie, the real secret of life everlasting.

CHAPTER 11

Maybe God
Is a Pure Red Iris

*W*e called him Mr. Harrison in the neighborhood—I don't remember his first name, if I ever knew it. He was my first teacher in the art of gardening and, as it turned out, in the art of living and dying. He never had much to say except when he was expounding on his plants, especially his irises. He lived just across the street from us in the suburban area north of Philadelphia where Carol and I were enjoying for the first time the luxury of owning our own home and not having to worry about what the landlord thought. Mr. Harrison was small, wizened actually, and well into retirement age. His face was always wreathed in an almost beatific smile, as if he were already enjoying the vision of God in paradise. Maybe he was, if God really is pleasant to look at. He and his wife were almost entirely self-sufficient on their three-fourths of an acre lot. Although both Carol and I had grown up on commercial farms, or perhaps because of that, this small homestead style of life in suburbia was new to us. Learning from Mr. Harrison, it became embarrassingly obvious how little we knew about horticulture, or agriculture for that matter, not to mention about the wild plants and animals that existed all around us.

Mr. Harrison had in earlier years worked as a groundskeeper, caretaker, and gardener on the estates of the wealthy. Now he grew all his own vegetables and fruit, fed table scraps to a few hens in return for eggs and meat, composted the animal manure and grass clippings for garden fertilizer—this all before it became trendy to do so. He had no activist tendencies toward organic gardening. This was just the way his father and grandfather had gardened and it worked well while not requiring much out-of-pocket money. He was always amazed at how what was just commonsense food production to him could become, in his old age, a cause célèbre. What fascinated me was how luxuriantly his plants grew without the commercial fertilizer that I had been taught had to be used, and how he could hybridize new strains of iris. He sold his iris bulbs as a small business. His dream was to develop a pure red blossom, which he said did not exist. If he succeeded, he said it would be worth a fortune. He did not seem to care about getting rich, however. I think he figured that the money angle made his project more interesting to people like me, which was true.

"What will you do if you produce a pure red iris?" I asked.

"Try to get one that is totally dark black," he answered without hesitation. Obviously the work itself, not the money, was his reward.

But the idea of possibly making a living from a very small acreage, which is all of a farm I thought I would ever be able to afford, intrigued me exceedingly. Could our own two acres do that for us? I watched Mr. Harrison work with his irises. Hand-pollinating to create new varieties was actually not difficult to do. One had to be meticulous about transferring pollen from the male anthers to the female stigma, making sure that other plants' pollen was excluded. But the operation wasn't difficult to master. Mr. Harrison put what looked like little bonnets over the flowers to keep out unwanted pollen. (One good book detailing how to do hybridizing today is *The Seed Underground* by Janisse Ray, published by Chelsea Green in 2012.) American society was simply not acculturated to this kind of work. We were programmed to buy our garden seeds and bulbs. Being able to buy stuff was the mark of success in our culture. It never occurred to us that we could develop our own new varieties.

"Do you know that in China, almost everybody knows how to hybridize plants, even children?" Mr. Harrison said. "It's part of the culture. They've traded their improved plants among themselves for centuries. They don't really need seed companies."

I was surprised. "For centuries?"

"Yes. Can you imagine American agriculture lasting that long? Ours will barely last another hundred years with the way we're going at it."

I was at the time a staff editor at *Farm Journal* magazine in Philadelphia and was imbued with the notion that chemical, piston-powered American agriculture was the promise of paradise. But this iris thing was very interesting.

Mr. Harrison followed a minimalist style of living. On three-fourths of an acre he had almost all the world he needed and was hardly reminded of the world he didn't need. He was content to stay at home, having in younger years, he said, "seen all the scenery I care to see." If he stood in the iris garden, with the pine trees, the chicken coop, and the house surrounding him, the whole outer world was almost totally blocked from view. Or rather, I think now, the outer world was condensed and concentrated into his tiny kingdom. The iris garden in late May was as beautiful as any tropical display of exotic plants. When the neighborhood lawnmowers were not destroying the peace of a Saturday morning, it was not hard to imagine that one was all alone there. He needed to buy very little to support his way of life. He had everything he wanted: his own food, his own well and rain barrels for water, his own combination of recreation and work, his own exotic scenery, his own business of selling iris bulbs. Television and books brought in as much of the outside world as he desired.

Other neighbors, Dick and Isabel, gardened avidly like we did, and had also discovered Mr. Harrison. Isabel asked him if he would teach her how to hybridize irises. He was pleased to do so and would have taught us, too. I wanted to try to grow a pure red iris, but, strangely, it was the kind of work neither Carol nor I thought we had time for yet. Carol did at least start to grow irises and did so from then on. Even years later, when I look at ours blooming in late May hundreds of miles from Mr. Harrison's world, I think of him. He had, by his example, unwittingly found a way to overcome mortality, at least a little.

Our three households made a model of what would be called, fifty years later, the new local food society. Dick and Isabel dreamed of being able to make a living with a little blueberry farm someday, and they already had a rather large planting of the fruit growing under screening at the back of their two-acre lot. Soon they started raising chickens just like Mr. Harrison did. Then Carol and I did, too. This was all before backyard chickens became fashionable again, as the practice had been before 1940. In fact our chickens caused some consternation to one neighbor for awhile. He got over it, though, when I offered him some free eggs. Another neighbor, after buying eggs from us the first time, called to say in a worried voice that there must be something wrong. "The yolks are so *orange*," she said. Carol assured her that was the way egg yolks were supposed to look.

The young people around us were fascinated. A couple of them spent considerable time recording our hens clucking and singing on tape. I was as amused watching them as they were amused watching the chickens. I had listened to singing hens most of my life and equated the sound with the contentedness I had felt as a child. But I would never have guessed that their singing could be a compelling curiosity to urban people. The whole notion of having food and music producers in the backyard, an idea as ancient as humans themselves, amazed them. As for myself, I was struck for the first time with the beauty of hen music that I had so long taken for granted.

Listening to our hens on tape, I began to wonder where music came from. I wondered again about beginnings and endings, about cause and effect, the subject that so puzzled me in my years of formal education. Both religious philosophers and physical scientists, choosing their favorite major premises, seemed so sure that they could deduce the truth by the logic of cause and effect. But it seemed so much more complicated to me. Which came first, the chicken or the egg? What part did the farmer play? How about the dog that chased away the raccoon that was about to kill the hen before she laid her eggs? What about the food the chicken ate? The tree that provided the wood that made the coop that sheltered the hens? The old nursery rhyme that Carol was reading to our children seemed to me a more effective treatise on the mysteries of cause and effect than Thomas Aquinas's *Summa Theologica*:

> *This is the farmer sowing the corn,*
> *that kept the cock that crowed in the morn,*
> *that waked the priest all shaven and shorn,*
> *that married the man all tattered and torn,*
> *that kissed the maiden all forlorn,*
> *that milked the cow with the crumpled horn,*
> *that tossed the dog*
> *that worried the cat*
> *that killed the rat*
> *that ate the malt*
> *that lay in the house that Jack built.*

Where or when did human music begin? Which came first, man or music? Did singing have a genetic cause oozing up out of our DNA, or did humans listen to sounds in nature and find, to their delight, that they could imitate them?

I asked Mr. Harrison what he thought about all this. He looked away, smiled, and replied: "Maybe the hens started to sing from listening to humans."

The suburban area we lived in brought me again to thinking about permanence, or rather the lack of permanence. All around us was evidence of impermanence. In our backyard, I was amazed to find an old, grassed-over dead furrow, which ran through the neighbors' backyards, too. But not being graduates of Warpole Creek, no one else living there knew that this straight, slight indentation in the lawns came from plowing at some long ago. I eventually made the acquaintance of a man in his nineties who lived in the area. When I told him about the dead furrow, he nodded. "Yes, where you live was a farm when I was young. I remember making hay there."

In the abandoned land between subdivisions where I liked to walk to catch the commuter train at the North Wales or Gwynedd Valley station, there were abandoned farmsteads still standing among new trees perhaps thirty years old. There was even a springhouse beside one ancient barn, quite usable. The place looked as if its owner had walked away maybe half a century ago and never come back. The land all around became covered with houses in which lived people who had no idea of what a springhouse was for, even though one of the nearby crossroads villages was named Springhouse.

The impermanence was everywhere. Walking around Springhouse one day, we noticed an old building across from the century-old inn where we had eaten lunch. We peeked in the crack in the door. Inside was a blacksmith shop, full of all the accoutrements of horseshoeing and iron forging, looking as if the owner had simply closed the door one day and never returned. To appreciate completely this veritable museum, visualize that hardly a stone's throw away, a new mall was being built. What made all this impermanence seem particularly mysterious is that when I'd ask people who lived in the area about these relics of yesterday, nobody seemed to know much. They were all newcomers, like us. The blacksmith shop, the abandoned barns, the springhouse, the hitching posts that unbelievably still stood at Gwynedd Valley's train station, were as much a part of the remote past to the people in the new subdivisions as the mound along Warpole Creek had been to us.

Every year, I could see how age was cutting down on Mr. Harrison's vigor. Came a day when he asked me if I would start his lawnmower for him. He couldn't pull the starting cord vigorously enough. Came another day when he butchered his chickens. After that he would hobble across the street and buy eggs from us, fishing coins out of a little black purse like my grandfather used to carry. We tried to give him eggs, but he was very insistent on paying for them. He actually was paying his way by giving me advice on my garden and trees. But buying them made him feel more at ease so I accepted the coins.

Even after his wife passed away, his smile did not at first dim. As he grew feebler, I would saunter over frequently to make sure he was all right. There were relatives who looked after him, too, but I could do it very handily and I wanted an excuse to visit and ask him gardening questions. In the afternoon he would be sitting in the shade next to his iris patch, sound asleep in his "garden chair." That seemed so neat to me, a man totally at peace with his world. I would try to slip away, hoping not to disturb him. If he were awake, or awoke at my approach, we would have discussions.

"What do you think about dying?" he once asked, abruptly.

I was taken aback. Dying was far removed from my focus in those days. Staying alive financially as a journalist, a profession I had no training in whatsoever, took all my attention. "What do you mean?"

"Wouldn't it be nice if I could just die sitting here asleep in my garden?"

Since it would be many years before I would have similar thoughts, I was too stunned to know what to say. Death was not a subject for polite conversation. It was like revealing how much money one had in the bank.

"They want to put me in an old folks' home, you know," he said, eyeing me closely.

Again, I did not know what to say.

"Can't you stop them?" Urgency slipped into his voice.

My mind was a jumble. There was no way I could inject myself into what was definitely, by the standards of the day, none of my business. But his words suggested something heavy with potent meaning. In a proper society where everyone in a neighborhood made a living locally and were always near at hand, we could have rallied around Mr. Harrison and taken care of him, sort of like the Amish did with their elderly. Retirement homes were hardly a necessity in a real community.

I looked down at the ground and mumbled, "I don't know how I could do that."

He nodded curtly. He did understand, of course. But the fear of being taken from his own little paradise, his source of comfort, joy, and security, made him willing to entertain any impossibility. "If I have to go there, I will starve myself to death anyway," he said. "I can do that here much more comfortably."

I fidgeted, actually alarmed a little by now. I had never put myself into the position of being old and helpless.

"Do you believe in heaven?" he asked. When I still didn't answer, he added, "Maybe this is heaven."

"And maybe God is a pure red iris," I said, the words coming without thinking from my mouth.

He smiled that huge smile of his again and as he turned away I thought I detected a faint, almost imperceptible nod of agreement.

One day Mr. Harrison disappeared. Just like that. We learned that he had been put in a retirement home, and we all agreed, trying to excuse a kind of guilt we felt, that "it was for the best." Not long afterward, we heard that he had died. I did not ask for details.

Soon after that, the iris garden and the pine grove disappeared and another house went up in their space. It seemed like such a desecration. At the same time, a salesman came to our door selling cemetery plots. I felt strangely alarmed, even insulted. I sent him away, almost rudely. How dare anyone think I was ever going to die? Only slowly becoming aware of how quickly everything changes everywhere all the time, I thought of death as something far, far away. Right now, I was only determined to find a place to live where new housing did not take precedence over old men, irises, and pine groves. I thought there really was such a place. I was still blinded by the idea of permanence.

CHAPTER 12

Resilience in Nature

*B*ack in the 1880s, the Sandusky River that flows through my neighborhood froze over in July and the end of the world sounded from every pulpit. Not many people knew then that a gigantic volcano, Krakatoa, had erupted in 1883 in Indonesia, throwing enough debris into the air to cloud the sun for several years. Even if they had been told that, I doubt many would have believed it. It was much more fun to preach that the world was ending. All they could do was fill the collection baskets in their churches with cash enough to persuade God to change his mind, which of course he did. Everyone was happy, especially the church ministers, because once more the bad weather passed, proving to those who already believed it that a beneficent God really did exist. And besides, the church really did need the money to put in a new furnace.

Imagine what would happen in these days of fearfulness, if such an event occurred now. Global freezing would be the great debate. We would be urged to burn more coal, oil, and gas to make global warming return.

The drought that much of the nation suffered during the summer of 2012 was said to be one of the worst ever in the Midwest and a sign of global warming. By August, I began to fall under the spell of classic doomsday chants about how maybe this was the beginning of the end. I had learned nothing from 1888 or, for that matter, from 1988 when it did not rain on our farm at all from April 11 until July 17. I was sure the end was nigh then, too. My parents were tempted by similar thoughts when bad years in the 1930s became almost the norm and we did not have global warming to blame.

Confronted with a frozen river in July today, Americans, in their present state of paranoia, would no doubt start committing suicide at even higher rates than we are now witnessing. Fervent Christians would be filling the church coffers with money, since the stuff is nearly worthless anyway, and fervent scientists would be suggesting rockets, the modern version of Noah's Ark, to transport them to some planet where the sun always shines except when rain is needed, and rain always falls, but not too much. (Interestingly, another Noah's Ark was actually being built in Kentucky in 2012. They say it is to lure tourists, but perhaps those evangelicals know something the rest of us don't. I wonder what a ticket will cost to ride out the next flood.)

While we justifiably fret about environmental decline, our worries obscure the amazing resilience of nature, which is evident all around us when we take the time to note it. I was much assured to learn, for example, that ginkgo trees survived the nuclear destruction of Hiroshima. In the aftermath of the Mount St. Helen's volcanic eruption in 1980 in the state of Washington, plants sprang back to life almost as quickly as the lava cooled. I also read (in Jane Goodall's book *Seeds of Hope* with Gail Hudson) how a Callery pear tree survived the 9/11 attack on the World Trade Center. Wild nature returned to Chernobyl after that nuclear devastation much faster than scientists had anticipated. Just recently *The New York Times Magazine* reported a wondrous example of natural resilience, a lowly jellyfish in Japan that possesses almost immortal life ("Forever and Ever" by Nathaniel Rich). In its natural environment—even in a petri dish if its environment is maintained there—this jellyfish will go on renewing itself physically forever, or at least until the next time ice freezes on the Sandusky in July. Even if attacked and reduced to near death, it will recompose and regenerate itself. I love what the scientist, Shin Kubota, who makes the jellyfish his major work, is quoted as saying: "Man is intelligent enough to achieve biological immortality. But we don't deserve it."

But I am hesitant to cite examples about which I have not had personal experience or contact. There are plenty of writers who have seen and written knowingly about the resilience of nature in faraway places. It is enough for me to watch weeds thrust their way up through the blacktop of a local parking lot to understand just how awesome is this process we call nature.

Wildlife is returning to my neighborhood much faster than expected, after increasing human population and commercial agriculture had done their best to destroy the natural landscape around me. The white-tailed deer had vanished completely by 1950 in our county. Now it has reached pestiferous numbers. Otters, wild turkeys, beavers, black bears, bobcats, coyotes, and eagles are all repopulating rural Ohio, which seemed only yesterday to be a giant baseball diamond planted to corn and soybeans. When a black walnut seedling came up in our asparagus patch several years ago, I cut it off at ground level, thinking that would get rid of it. (Walnut roots exude juglone, a chemical compound that can kill asparagus.) It grew right back, of course. I cut it off again and again it grew back. I got curious and started keeping count. Over the course of several years, I decapitated that stubborn seedling fourteen times and still it grew back. In exasperation and curiosity, I made a little fire of dead leaves over it to burn it into extinction. It grew back again. I had to dig out the roots to kill the seemingly fragile little seedling.

Trees are way ahead of people in the effort to achieve immortality. Sycamores, like the one I can see out my office window, were proliferating when the dinosaurs roamed the earth. A sycamore along the Sandusky River in my home village of Upper Sandusky was a favorite gathering spot all through the late 1800s, even in the year the ice froze in July. It was thought by local people to be the largest sycamore east of the Mississippi, but I've heard that story before. A photo in a local history book shows that it had sported seven trunks by 1900, each quite large, that had grown up around the first ancient trunk, which evidently had rotted away. The tree was estimated at being over two centuries old. Folklore says that the owner of the land where the tree grew, suspicious (or jealous) of young people frolicking, picnicking, drinking, and consorting in its shade, tried to burn it down. Steeped in immortality, the sycamore declined to cooperate. It was only in 1903, during a bad storm, that it finally blew over. But rest assured, there were still many sycamores shading the river in my days of frolicking along its banks, and I have a hunch they will still be there when the dinosaurs come back.

Most of us are surprised to learn that there are more forested acres now in the eastern United States than there were a hundred years ago. I have no trouble believing that because I have lived in the woods a long time and have seen firsthand the relentless power of vegetative growth. Trees advance on me on all sides, and as I grow older and feebler I recognize how difficult it is to hold them at bay without a forest fire or seven hundred gallons of Roundup. We think of trees as slow-growing plants, but when I turn my back on a fence line or woodland edge for hardly more than one year, the saplings spring up and head for the sun. Even faster are the weeds and brush that precede them. I was amazed to see that, left to its own devices, a multiflora rose bush can quadruple in size in one summer. Under the brush, the tree seedlings start, and in five years here they come, above the weedy growth, gaining the sunlight, mounting to the sky.

I used to worry about the almost constant reports of tree diseases threatening to eradicate one species or another. Gypsy moths were ruining the eastern forests (which were regrowing after the original clearing of mountain woodlands by humans). The forest survived both of these threats quite well. Then Dutch elm disease was sending American elms to oblivion, or so we thought. Now the elm trees are growing back—I can see a score of them in our little grove just out the window. Today the emerald ash borer is killing all the white ash trees, or so we are told—I can see dead ashes out the same window. But I can also see literally hundreds of little white ash seedlings that will likely outlast the borer, just as the elm seedlings outlasted the fungal disease carried by a bark beetle from Europe. The USDA Forest Service just released a report indicating that the prediction about the end of the western pine forests from another bark beetle was a bit premature. The number of dead and dying trees has slowed down considerably for the very logical reason that there are fewer trees for the beetles to eat and so the number of beetles is in decline, too. The news is good for the recovery of the pines, says the Forest Service, but adds that these things go in cycles and new pests and diseases are sure to come.

That is how humans describe what happens, not the forest talking. The human mind sees cycles because we think in terms of beginnings and endings, of causes and effects, of time passing. But the forest acts only in the everlasting NOW. Death is not an ending but the beginning of something else. Trees do not come and go in preordained cycles, but endlessly in sporadic episodes. I struggle for the right words to describe true eternity, but can't find them. Trees do not speak in words. As Eric Toensmeier writes in his book *Paradise Lot* (Chelsea Green, 2013): "[Succession] does not have a beginning, middle, and end. There is no point you can call a climax, and it doesn't happen uniformly across a large piece of land. Nor can its outcome be precisely predicted. Rather succession arises from a disturbance to a given *patch* of land."

Right now there is much hand-wringing over diseases that are attacking oak trees, especially white oak. My hands do not wring in this regard as much as they would have a few years ago. I daily confer with a congregation of oaks outside my door, and they assure me that they will be around a whole lot longer than I will be. Two of them are burr oaks, five are white oaks, three more are black oaks, and there's one each of pin oak and red oak. They are all somewhere between one and two hundred years old. There are several threats to their continued existence as species, but again, *threat* is not a tree word. As long as climate dictates trees, trees in one form or another will be here, and if I could live another century or two, I'd cover all bets that the oaks will be here still.

Oaks won't grow in the heavy shade of the maples that have shouldered their way into the grove, so the oaks are threatened that way. Before the arrival of Europeans, one way nature took care of this "problem," so the foresters tell me, was with fire. It appears that humans deliberately started some of the fires. Wherever one finds a stand of white or burr oaks, it means fire paved the way. Humans were smart enough to make use of the oaks' resilience. White oaks, particularly burr oak, can endure fire to some extent, and when flames sweep through the forest, these oaks survive and drop acorns, which then rise up and get a head start on more shade-tolerant tree species. Once they have the sun, the oaks rule.

But I rather think that the oaks survived and will continue to survive because they develop in a mosaic of patches, each patch fending for itself, as Toensmeier says. A few trees always survive various diseases and insect attacks because they outlive threats to them. Oaks are steeped in the skills of survival. Their acorns are food for a growing population of animals, and for awhile I was tempted to think the proliferating wildlife would eat too many, that none would be left to propagate new trees. I have paid particular attention to the white oak tree right next to the house because in the last two winters a herd of about seven deer have come nightly to nose out the acorns under it when the snow is not deep. Several families of squirrels and chipmunks feast on these acorns, too. Blue jays and wild turkeys, now on the rise, eat their share, although the latter are too shy (I think) to come this close to the house. In any event, I was absolutely sure no acorns would be left to start new trees last spring. Unbelievably, I found fifty new seedlings in April before I grew tired of counting. We humans do not grasp the efficiency of nature because to us it seems so inefficient. A mature oak tree will drop thousands of acorns in a good bearing year. If only one sprouts and grows every century, that is enough to keep the species alive and ready for the favorable year when hundreds of new trees will start.

The tenacity of a white oak acorn is particularly astounding. It falls in October here. Within a couple of weeks, lying on the soil surface, it can put down a root five inches long. I have examined acorns that were half-eaten by parasitical worms *still* putting down this root that quickly. In spring, rootlets jump out all along that first fall sprout, and the new seedling is off for the sun.

The resilience of nature is especially noticeable after a bad drought like the one we suffered through in 2012. The bluegrass and white clover that dominate our pastures wilted away by June, and some areas turned into bare dirt by the end of August. But when it began to rain again, the bluegrass just went wild. It filled the bare spots in no time and shouldered out the new fescue that also was trying to grow. By November I had a thick sward of pasture, much more than the sheep could keep up with, enough to keep them until January when the snow was not too deep. In fact, as it turned out, the sheep still were nibbling at the bluegrass in the following March, and by April the new growth was coming on. In other words, while I had lost grazing in June, July, and August, I gained it back in September, October, November, and December, and even some through the winter because there was deep snow only once. This is another example of why I almost scream in protest and frustration every time I hear a pasture expert declare that bluegrass is not "desirable" forage because it goes dormant in dry late summers.

My pastures are also telling me that there are better ways to approach immortality than the annual cultivation that humankind is pursuing at the moment. If life everlasting is ever going to be achieved, we need to listen better to nature. There are everlasting ways to get our food, even in a year of drought. We do not need to build arks or rockets, but rather fields of perennial plants. Perhaps some etymologist of the future will discover that the old books of the Bible have been translated incorrectly. It was perhaps not an ark that Noah built, but a highland perennial pasture.

Chapter 13

The Parsnip Way to Everlasting Life

*T*he parsnip is a mystifying vegetable. It has been around since at least the days of ancient Rome, is almost always present on food market shelves, and legions of seemingly invisible people pledge their undying love for it. They must be invisible because I never see anyone actually buying a parsnip or eating one at any table except our own, and that was only for one season. The brotherhood of the parsnip must be an ancient, secret society whose members share their addiction and recipes only with one another lest the whole world find out how good the root can be and start a run on it at the grocery store.

I have always felt a compelling, almost eerie connection to parsnips because the same year I planted them my mother died. During the whole winter that followed, whenever I looked at my parsnip patch, mounded over with leaves, I thought of her grave. At first the reminder was sharp with pain, but digging up the gnarly roots in late winter somehow soothed me a little, as if unearthing them kept Mother alive in some strange way. I wrote a poem about it:

ROOTS

"You plant them early in July," she told me,
The son who didn't know the pleasures of the old days.
"Come February the frost will take out all the bitterness.
Fixed right, they make the first good eating of the year."

So I planted parsnips and planned, come February
To take them to her to fix right, for who else could?
We'd eat them together, relishing old-fashioned ways
That meant nothing except to our kind.

But February did not come for her, just November
With a cruel coldness that was not the weather only,
That was the weather least of all.
The green tops of the parsnips fell and died—their time.

A pile of leaves now rest within my garden,
Beneath which parsnip roots lie snug against the cold.
I stand and stare today, too long, at that low mound.
It looks like Momma's grave.

A last and tenuous link between her soul and mine,
Between old days dying and new ones yet to live.
Between an old woman saying goodbye,
And a young man taking root.

But who will cook those parsnips come February,
Who will eat them relishing rich old ways?
And will the frost by then
Take out all the bitterness?

My sorrow drove me to learn more about parsnips, as if somehow that would allow me to keep her alive in some strange way. In my own limited experience, the seeds were slow to germinate, so that by the time the plants were up the weeds had gained a head start. But once growing above the weeds, they were invincible. We cooked the roots about like we cooked carrots and found them edible enough if lathered with butter, which of course is a good way to make anything taste better, even cardboard. The "literature" on vegetables that was available to me had little to say about parsnips, and what I did find was contradictory. For example, Peter Henderson's book *Gardening for Profit*, first published in 1867, advised market gardeners to forgo parsnips because they were not profitable enough. Then, in something of an about-face, he told about a year when a shortage of parsnips in the market sent him and his workers to a frozen field to pry them up "with crowbars, picks and wedges." From a little more than half an acre, he sold eight hundred dollars' worth of the root. Remember, these were 1860 dollars.

In the 1990s I finally found and visited in Indiana a true advocate of parsnips, John McMahan, who wrote and published in 1995 a delightfully down-home little book he called *Farmer John Outdoors*, in which he had only praise for the parsnip. "I wouldn't want to be without it," he wrote. "It is the lazy gardener's vegetable par excellence." He talked of roots eighteen inches long and as big around as a man's forearm. He believed that parsnips had lost their appeal for awhile in the 1940s, '50s, and '60s, but were on a comeback.

I have a hunch that he was right because many years later, in 2012 to be exact, I remarked on my blogsite rather negatively about the taste of parsnips. Readers irascibly contradicted me. While some admitted that one must be rather hungry to enjoy them, many others told me in no uncertain terms that I just didn't know how to "fix them right," as my mother had put it. They suggested a variety of ways to make them wonderfully tasty:

sliced and roasted with a bit of olive oil; roasted and buttered; mashed with potatoes or turnips; sautéed until caramelized; and included in stews and soups. One respondent did caution that the parsnip can easily overwhelm the flavor of other vegetables if not used in moderation. Roasting, all agreed, brings out a unique sweetness in the root. It is this sweetness, which only comes after the root stays in the cold ground over winter (or is refrigerated for awhile if dug in the fall), that makes it tasty to its devotees. In fact, wine has traditionally been made from parsnips. If you're thirsty enough for alcohol, you can make wine out of anything, except maybe granite rocks.

Parsnips are grown much like their relative, carrots. Freezing the seed or soaking it in water for twenty-four hours before planting is supposed to help it germinate faster. The fresher the seed, the better. But, as if to prove their contrariness, parsnips will reseed themselves quite readily. This ability has led to a unique and intriguing practice for those who like plants that can take care of themselves. Some growers keep a permanent patch of parsnips, letting some of them reseed every year on their own. The plants grow to about five feet and blossom handsomely, I am told.

The leaves and stems of parsnips contain furanocoumarin, a somewhat toxic organic compound that not only can cause a painful twisting of the tongue when one tries to say the word, but also protects the plant from bugs. The roots, as far as I can find out, do not contain the compound, so in effect the parsnip comes to you with its own built-in insecticidal protection.

If parsnips could talk or write, they could provide us with a formula for how to attain life everlasting in the garden, if not elsewhere. In an interview, Mr. Parsnip would have plenty of advice, honed by centuries of survival.

"First, cultivate an independent kind of ornery reliability that will draw admiration from everyone, except maybe politicians and church authorities who want their subjects to stand before them with bowed heads in abject dependence. Learn how to survive winter in frozen ground, or, for you humans, how to survive economic recession in comfort. We parsnips not only know how to endure frozen soil, but how to taste better because of it. Then make sure that your seed will drop and sprout of its own accord if necessary to guarantee something close to perpetual life.

"Second, develop a distinctive personality like we parsnips do, with a taste only appreciated by the few rather than by the many. You want to appeal to the discerning minority, not the herd-like majority, which is always susceptible to the moneychangers. If you are too desirable as a plant, the gene manipulators will bioengineer you into oblivion.

"Third, don't try to look too pretty in public. Everybody is dressing up fancy these days, so if you follow suit (no pun intended), you'll just be ignored. Or worse, you will be asked to head up a fund-raiser. If you look sort of bony, weathered, and wrinkled, like us parsnips, some master chef will get interested and make you famous."

CHAPTER 14

------- ◆ -------

The Day the Pigs Must Die

*W*e raise our farm animals with loving care, grow quite fond of them, put our lives at risk to save theirs if necessary, and then we kill and eat them. Growing up in an agrarian culture, I never saw or felt any contradiction involved with this. Eating meat was a necessary part of life. What in all of creation could satisfy like tenderloin and fresh sausage on butchering day? Or pork chops all year long? Or ham after it was salted, sugared, smoked, and hung in the smokehouse to cure for several months? These were the delights of life and, at least for children, butchering day, attended by a large gathering of family and neighbors to share the work involved, was more like a party. My most vivid memories are of butchering day at my grandfather's farm. I can still see Grandmother and her sisters sitting in the kitchen, each with a wooden board on her lap, on which they were "cleaning guts," the phrase used to describe scraping the offal out of the pig intestines so the latter, scrupulously cleaned and turned inside out, could be used as casing for the sausage. This was not a pleasant job, and those women were always wearing, in my memory, tightly tied headbands because of severe headaches that afflicted them during the stress of butchering day. As they talked to one another, they were often crying, which I thought was in reaction to the grisly, smelly job—sometimes there were roundworms in the defecation they were scraping out of the intestines—but when I asked my mother about that in later years, she turned away slightly and said curtly: "Some of them had husbands that would make anybody want to cry."

Carol actually enjoys scraping guts, she says, or the bit of it that she was allowed to do as a child. She can describe in detail how to push the crap out of the small intestines on the board and how the cleaned gut was turned cleverly inside out by folding the end of a length of gut up a little and holding it while pouring water into the fold. The gut telescoped itself inside out. I wonder who figured that out. I wonder even more why sausages were put into links in the first place.

Eventually my own turn came to continue the long tradition of butchering pork, to be the boss of the butchering, which is why, this cold early-winter morning, I am resolutely headed for the barn trying to look happy about it all. At least we have long ago dispensed with the gut-cleaning business, saving our sausage as frozen patties instead of in links. My son, son-in-law, and several other family members are with me, affecting bravado to hide the distaste for the job we all feel. We have abandoned the tradition of strong alcoholic beverages on butchering day, which is how earlier generations often got through the job. Most of the "womenfolks" stay at the house to avoid witnessing the killing, and some of them discourage their children from watching it, too, although there have been the usual discussions about how "they might as well learn the real world now as later," or "if you want to eat meat, you need to learn how it gets to the table." The children themselves, the first generation raised mostly within the confines of the computer screen, react differently to the butchering, according to their personalities. Unlike children in my generation, who could go through the bloodiest butchering without flinching, the "new generation" is mostly full of repugnance at the blood and gore. Those who have enjoyed scratching the pigs, Matilda and Petunia, behind the ears look at me in angry bewilderment. I can only say, with eyes downcast, that "if you want to eat meat, someone has to do the dirty work."

The killing is the worst part of butchering day. Once a hog is dead, cutting up the meat does not seem so immediately bound to the taking of life—it's more like dissecting a frog in high school biology class. My son and I do the actual killing. He shoots them with a .22 revolver, the gun held close to the pig's unsuspecting head so as to ensure accuracy, the bullet going exactly in the middle of the frontal skull but an inch lower than a line drawn mentally between the eyes. He strongly dislikes this job, I know, but the other part of the killing is even more distasteful. Two can do the job better than one. The bullet stuns the pig and it drops like a rock. I roll it on its side just enough so I can "stick it," plunging a knife through its throat and into its jugular vein. If I do it correctly, the blood immediately gushes out. Sometimes I have to wiggle the tip of the knife around a bit to get the blood to gush. It is not only loathsome but dangerous because the hog's feet may start thrashing about when the knife goes in and the pig's hooves can catch the slaughterer's hand and bruise it, or even catch the arm and drive the withdrawn knife into the slaughterer's body. It has happened. As the hog writhes and squeals in the throes of death, I understand why a bottle of whiskey so often accompanies butchering day. I also understand why one of my best friends is a vegetarian. He has no lofty ideas about not eating meat; he just points out that a meatless diet makes homestead life so much easier.

It takes a minute or two for the hog to bleed out. In the olden days the blood was caught in a pan to be turned into "blood pudding," but that is another part of traditional butchering that we don't follow. Once the animal quits writhing about, the stress drains out of me, too. The rest of the job is far from easy, but the lifeless carcass is less stressful to deal with. First I cut the skin behind the hog's back legs, baring the tendons there, and slide a meat hook under these tendons. The other ends of the two hooks are set into notches on a wooden tripod, the legs of which are each about ten feet long. With several strong men working together, the tripod is slowly pushed into an upright position, bearing the weight of the two-hundred-or-so-pound carcass. It is a tricky maneuver with one or two men pushing on one of the tripod legs while other men make sure the other two tripod legs bite into the ground, not slip, as the carcass is elevated. Once the tripod is up, the hog carcass hangs head-down amid the three legs, handy for skinning and gutting.

Traditionally, before being hung on the tripod, a hog carcass was scalded and hair removed with metal scrapers. Several strong men were necessary to hoist or drag the carcass onto a raised platform and then slide it in and out of a barrel of scalding-hot water. The barrel was lashed in a slanted position onto the edge of the raised platform, the idea at all times being to move the carcass without having to lift it completely since the hog might weigh three hundred or more pounds. After several dunkings in the barrel, the carcass was attacked by as many as four men, each scraping away furiously at the hair with hog scrapers. There is know-how involved. The scalding water must be hot enough but not too hot, and the pig dunked in the water several times with a bit of airing between the dunkings. I once asked an old farmer how he knew when the water was just hot enough. Without hesitation he replied that he stuck his finger in and out of the water in rapid succession. When he could stand to do that three times, but no more, the water was ready.

The reason for scalding off the hog's hair was so that every bit of the fat under the hide could be saved for making lard. But after suffering through quite a few hog scaldings in younger years, I had decided we could get all the lard we wanted by skinning the hog instead of scalding and scraping. We think lard is as necessary an ingredient to cooking as our ancestors did, but wasting a little that is left when the hide is skinned off isn't that important in these days of plenty. So now, with the carcass suspended from the tripod, we cut off the outer skin and hair with knives, starting at the back legs and skinning on down to the throat, peeling the skin off almost as if it were a garment. We are far from professionals at this job but get it done eventually.

Then the carcass is opened by slitting a line directly down the middle of the belly and chest to empty out the intestines, stomach, lungs, and other non-meat organs. If done correctly, almost all of it comes out in one huge jelly-like mass. To start the slit, I first cut out around the hog's tail and then down the belly a few inches, enough to get my hands inside to tie the colon closed so manure can't squeeze out during the gutting process. There is a thin bone directly between the back legs that has to be severed, too. It is a fairly soft bone that I cut through by tapping the back edge of the butchering knife held blade-down against it with a hammer. I don't think written words can accurately describe this (or other fine points of butchering), but I feel compelled for some strange reason to try to describe it. We all say, before the day is over, that meat has to taste very good indeed for us to do the butchering. But then there is a division of opinion. Some say that humans are genetically driven to eat meat and that, without it, the species would degenerate over several generations. Others say that, as omnivores, we could live without meat, but it just tastes too good to give up. I bore everyone by saying what I always do: The food chain is a vast dining room around which sit the eating being eaten.

"If some of those city people were watching us right now, they'd be horrified," someone says.

"Yeah. But they think it's okay in nature when a bunch of wolves pull down a cow and tear it apart while it is still alive," says another.

The tricky part when opening the carcass is to keep from cutting into the intestines, which press closely against the belly skin. If the intestines are cut, the waste material inside will ooze out, making the whole messy, smelly job even messier and smellier. I keep my left hand moving along between belly organs and skin as I cut with my right hand. This way, I'd cut my hand before I cut into an intestine. I always keep a bucket of clean water handy to wash down the carcass and my hands as I proceed. I separate the liver and the heart from the other organs after the whole business tumbles out into a wheelbarrow. Then I sever the head completely from the body. Wastefully, we throw the head away for the buzzards. Proper butchering requires cutting out the jowl meat and tongue for eating, too, but no one in our family will eat tongue.

The carcass is then cut in half in a straight line down the backbone. I use a handsaw. Electric ones are easier but of course cost more money. Either way, one must saw carefully so that the vertebrae are dissected exactly in the middle. Strong, younger men then carry the two sides of the carcass up to the garage where they are hung by the meat hooks still in the tendons of the back feet, to cool out. The cooling can be done right on the tripods if depredation by dogs or wild animals is not a problem. Either way, we think hanging for a few days in a cold, airy place is necessary to good-tasting meat. The body heat gets completely out of the meat in a relatively short time and a bit of aging occurs, and this is the reason home-butchered pork invariably seems to taste better than meat that comes from some commercial butchering operations where the cooling may last only a few hours.

That means our meat hangs until the next weekend, while I worry that if the weather gets too cold it might freeze. Butchering in early winter or late winter, we have never had that happen, although on occasion I have covered the hanging carcasses with old blankets to prevent it.

Then the meat is cut up into its traditional pieces: hams, ribs, tenderloins, shoulders, bacon, and so on. This is generally skilled work done by professional meat cutters, but on the old-fashioned farm some of us learned how to do it. Removing the sides of bacon from the ribs is the hardest task, I think. Also knowing precisely the right place to separate the hams and shoulders from the carcass takes experience. Plenty of books give directions, but I've learned that if you goof a little, it doesn't matter all that much for home consumption. Less-skilled family members trim excess fat to be used for lard from the meat, and slice up stray pieces of meat not usually part of the traditional pieces, to be ground up into sausage. Cutting up the meat is the more enjoyable part of the butchering. Traditionally, the workers sit around a long table, trimming meat and fat, often passing around a bottle of whiskey or two. The conversation grows quite lively.

"Henry, don't forget to save the chitlins. That ole guy down my road especially asked for them."

"What's chitlins?"

"Mountain oysters." Giggles all up and down the table.

"Nope. Chitlins is gut and stomach lining, not mountain oysters."

"Well, what's mountain oysters?"

"Hog balls to you." More laughing.

"Better than brains and sweetbreads."

"Blood pudding is the worst."

"You gotta know how to fix that stuff. You salt it good and sew it up in a stomach lining and hang it up the fireplace chimley for awhile. Mighty good eatin' then."

"Glad you think so. Means more pork chops and ribs for me."

We cook small amounts of fat on the stove, but in a real traditional butchering, lard rendering is done outside in a huge iron pot over an open fire. The chunks of fat turn brown as the lard is rendered out of them; finally the cooked chunks go into a lard press, where the last bit of juice is pressed from them. What remains are called cracklings, which resemble very greasy potato chips.

"Those things aren't good for you, you know," I say to a bystander who is joyously munching cracklings out of the lard pot. "Very bad for the cholesterol."

He stares at me, expressionless, pops another crackling in his mouth, and replies: "Cholesterol be damned."

After the hot lard was emptied from the iron pot on the embers, my father in the olden days would toss in a couple of handfuls of popcorn. Soon the corn would start popping and the first few kernels would fly out of the pot. But then the corn would pop so fast that it covered the surface enough so that the popped kernels stayed contained within the pot. It was a magical thing to behold. And no popcorn could taste any better. Nor any pie taste better than one cooked with the lard from that pot. Yes. Cholesterol be damned.

I wonder if our repugnance over killing animals for food is but another manifestation of our fear of dying and being eaten ourselves. The central celebration of Christian religion comes from the Last Supper: "This is my body; this is my blood." I long ago rejected the crazy notion that bread and wine can actually become body and blood as Catholicism holds. But just maybe this doctrine, this "transubstantiation" of bread and wine into the body and blood of "Christ the Savior," is a bit of genius, interpreted correctly. All bodies, plant and animal, are constantly being killed, eaten, and transformed into other bodies. Maybe the words attributed to a "Savior" allegorically express the deepest truth of all: "This bread is my body, take ye and eat."

CHAPTER 15

Buzzard Bait

A most unlikely bird arrived at the bird feeder outside our kitchen window recently, a turkey vulture, alias *Cathartes aura*, or what we call a buzzard. It never actually came right up to the bird feeder but sat a few feet away on a tree branch and stared stonily into the kitchen window at us. Nothing can stare as stonily as a buzzard. Its black body with a garish bald red head qualified it as the ugliest bird ever to strut on nature's stage. On the tree branch, it kept its wings partially spread, which gave it a haunting, hunched-over, witch-like aura of ghostliness.

What was it doing, coming so close to human habitation? Buzzards don't like humans unless they are dead, and I know they don't eat sunflower seeds. This one was well aware that we were watching it. If I so much as wiggled a finger, its wings would rise a little farther into the air, prepared to heave its eagle-sized body aloft. But something emboldened it to stay put. The answer finally dawned on me. Close to the bird feeder on the deck, there was a plastic container in which we save food scraps for the chickens.

We had been butchering broilers the day before, and Carol had put the last bits of stray gut and skin that she had cleaned from the chicken parts into it. The stench was overwhelming, but with the lid on the container, we couldn't smell it. The buzzard evidently could, even from high up in the sky. Its powerful sense of smell had drawn it down, down, down, to our very doorstep. Now perplexed and having no instinct to deal with plastic containers, it just sat there, waiting to see what might develop. Buzzards are very good at waiting to see what happens next. I was reminded of an ancient bit of folklore that lingers in a local village. The buzzards like to roost, so it is said, in the big tree that hovers over the funeral home. Could it be true that they can smell the cadavers?

When I am out working in the fields, there are always buzzards wheeling high in the sky above me, and I like to imagine that they are patiently waiting for me to die. Maybe they can smell death already settling in my old bones. But they circled above me even when I was young. Maybe they are just hoping. Most likely, after eons of experience, the knowledge is sealed in their genes: Something down on the earth's surface below them is soon going to die. Buzzards have built-in job security. Something is always dying.

As haunting a scene as I've encountered anywhere in the world happened in my pastures one morning. Walking over the brow of a hill, I suddenly came upon a row of fence posts with a buzzard perched atop each one. Six of them. Closer inspection revealed that more buzzards were on the ground, tearing up a dead sheep carcass with gluttonous abandon. The ones on the posts were waiting their turn, and acting as sentinels, too, I suppose. As I walked toward them, very slowly so as not to scare them away, they spread and raised their wings, preparing to fly off if I came too close. Those wings can span six feet from tip to tip, and a row of buzzards so poised was awesomely eerie, beyond anything I'd ever seen in nature or even in movies. Think of the mythical Thunderbird of American Indian folklore. Now think of six of them staring at you at eye level from totem-pole fence posts fifty feet away. Now turn on the sound of six more of them on the ground, snarling at one another as they rip the guts out of a dead sheep.

Sometimes buzzards can gorge so wantonly on a carcass that they can't fly. They will disgorge some the contents of their stomachs so that they can get airborne. I have not seen them do that, but my father warned me many years ago to steer clear of a certain hollow log in the woods. A buzzard was nesting there. He said buzzards, to protect their young, will vomit on intruders and that the smell is far worse than skunk spray.

The reason buzzards fascinate me is that all this dramatic awesomeness is almost always near at hand in the countryside, almost as common as robins, but people rarely seem to notice them. It is another example of human shortsightedness. To gain attention, writers go off to faraway places with strange names like Komodo Island in Indonesia in search of dragons, or into the wilds of Tasmania perhaps to glimpse one of its devils, when they might well look deeply into their backyards and see even more breathtaking wonders. Buzzards are as much a part of the American landscape as oak trees and squirrels. Their natural range stretches from the southern tip of South America far into Canada. Logically, there is every reason to think that they should be almost extinct by now because they are so big and vulnerable and often sit precariously close to traffic along roadsides while eating the carrion that automobiles leave in their wake. But they are actually growing in numbers.

One of the paintings of artist Andrew Wyeth is of buzzards high up in the sky (*Soaring*). I was intrigued that someone so famous should spend his time painting buzzards. So I asked him about it. He was fascinated by the big birds, he said, not only because they could have such great visual impact, but because humans did not seem to take much notice of them. That anomaly prompted him to paint them. Since he only saw them from the underside as they floated majestically on the sky currents, he wondered what a buzzard looked like topside. Enlisting the aid of Karl Kuerner, his neighbor on whose farm he practically grew up, they used a placenta from a newborn calf as bait and trapped one of the big birds. Then they spread-eagled it, or rather spread-vultured it, out to its widest six-foot wingspan, and the artist sketched it from above. In the painting, the soaring buzzards are seen that way, from above, looking down on the Kuerner farm.

Karl Kuerner's grandson, also Karl, became a successful artist, too, and a close friend of mine because he helped me gain an audience with the world-famous Wyeth. Karl is fascinated by buzzards more than anyone I know, and there are plenty of them above the Kuerner farm after a century of cattle and sheep living and dying on the farm's pasture fields. Karl paints almost exclusively on the Kuerner family farm and, not surprisingly, two of his better-known paintings are of buzzards. One of them is startling: a rendering of a buzzard sitting calmly in his wife's lap (*A Buzzard in Her Lap*). The story all started one morning when they found a buzzard sitting on the roof of their house. Since it had a band on its leg, they figured it had escaped from some kind of bird sanctuary. It did not seem particularly afraid of them. When it lingered, they put out some raw bacon on the deck and the buzzard came right down and ate it. Eventually it would eat out of their hands. The Kuerners have a way with animals of all kinds; wild deer eat out of Karl's hand, too. The buzzard, whom they called Buzz, became a pet and a lovable one at that, something no one would expect for such a forbidding-looking bird. So playful did it become, in fact, that sometimes when Louise sat on the deck it would hop up on the railing close to her and pass its beak through her hair, as if preening!

(There is a creepy coincidence here that my mind won't let go of no matter how I try to dissuade it. Louise passed away a couple of years ago from cancer, and though the buzzard in her lap or running its beak through her hair preceded that event by several years, I thought of her when the buzzard visited our bird feeder while I was fighting cancer. Could buzzards sense . . . no, no, Gene, don't be ridiculous.)

Buzz hung around the Kuerners' house all summer, leaving in the evening to roost with other neighborhood vultures and coming back every morning for a handout of raw bacon. "Once I found a dead mouse in the barn that somehow the cats had ignored, so I brought it to the house for Buzz," Karl recalled recently. "That big bird just plummeted down from the roof, took that stinking mouse from my hand, tore it apart with a furious intensity it never showed in its relationship to us, and ate it."

Karl had become enamored of buzzards as a boy on a farm. Another of his paintings (*November Winds*) depicts them gliding high in the sky. "I watch them through binoculars," he says today. "There is no bird as graceful as they are. It is just unbelievable how majestically and effortlessly they can soar. On the ground, they are so ungainly, but in the air so elegant. Buzz would descend on the house with great speed, pull up at the last second, stick his big feet out, and land on the roof with a loud clumsy thump. I threw some spoiled meat out for the flock on the pasture hill next to my studio. It was amazing how quickly they came out of the sky. It was like football players diving on a fumble."

One day he saw a buzzard literally sitting on the back of one of his sheep, with other buzzards nearby. He took a photo of the scene, knowing no one would have believed him otherwise. But none of us shepherds were surprised. Perhaps buzzards know, as we know, that sheep just love to die and will go out of their way to do so. My sister had some sheep grazing in her orchard once, where her children had tied a rope swing to an apple branch. As unbelievable as it seems, one of the sheep managed to hang itself on the swing.

The most dramatic buzzard in Karl's life is the one that hangs from his dining room and from which you can look down into his studio on the lower floor. It looks very much like Wyeth's buzzards do in *Soaring*. "I actually had that painting in mind when I talked a friend and student of mine who is a wood-carver into carving that buzzard for me. It is life-sized and life-like, and it reminds me always of how closely life and death are linked on the farm."

Yes! Nothing symbolizes better the reality of the farm and garden, bustling with life but always near to death. The buzzard was the perfect totem of that clash of life and death: a visionary Thunderbird, breathtakingly beautiful in the sky, fearsomely ugly on the ground; life and death clothed in mordant black feathers and fiery-alive red head.

On a practical level, buzzards do very beneficial work, cleaning up dead animals for us at no cost. But, once more, we humans try to thwart nature's wisdom. We make laws against letting animals rot out in the field. We say we do it out of fear of disease, but we really do it in an effort to avoid the unpleasantness of it all. Rendering factories make good use of dead animals, no doubt about it, but out in the countryside when a cow or sheep dies and hauling the carcasses to some distant rendering plant isn't practical, society says that dead stuff must be buried, and in some places you can get fined if you don't. Yet buzzards can make short work of such a carcass. They swoop in almost immediately—prefer, in fact, fresh carrion before the stench gets really offensive. A flock of them will clean up a dead sheep, leaving only the bones, in a day. The number of them circling high in the sky seems few, but they have some sort of remarkable communication system among them. When the ones directly above carrion drop down to eat, the ones a quarter mile away see them and move in. The buzzards another quarter mile away note the congregation and they head for the party, too. I've seen as many as forty or fifty of the big birds arrive on the scene in an hour or so, and before very long only the carcass's bones are left. Where buzzards (and crows and even eagles) do their best work is along highways where roadkill is always plentiful.

Unfortunately, buzzards from more northerly states migrate to at least the Ohio River Valley, so their services aren't available all year round where I live. They start leaving my farm in late October and return in early March. Much ado is made of their return to Ohio: The event supposedly always occurs on March 14 in Hinckley, Ohio. I know from personal experience that they can arrive there as much as a week earlier or later than that, but it gives journalists something to write about. Whatever the exact date, their return is one of the first sure signs of spring, and when they leave, the first unpleasant sign of approaching winter. I have seen buzzards gather near Newark, Ohio, in great numbers, covering whole hillsides in black, another awesome sight that the natives seem to ignore as the birds wait for the right currents of air from the south to wing their way farther north. During these flock gatherings, people in towns like Newark have nothing good to say about the big birds because they tend to roost in streetside trees and cover limbs and sidewalks with manure.

We have made it a cultural commandment to bury dead animals when in many instances it would be so much easier to encourage more buzzards. But one such seemingly logical thought leads to another, much more disturbing. Could I carry the dead body of a loved one out onto the hillside and let the buzzards devour it? In that moment of truth, I know why people try to ignore buzzards: Why they tell stories of buzzards that pecked the eyes out of sleeping humans, even though the known facts declare that turkey vultures never go after living animals (though black vultures do). The thought of buzzards and maggots eating human bodies drives us to underground burial and, since that won't prevent worms and microbes from doing the same thing, to elaborate caskets and tombs and mausoleums, all in a vain attempt to prevent our bodies from natural and beneficial decay. Again I ask myself: Could I lay the dead body of my dear wife out in the pasture for the buzzards? Nature and even scientific logic says that that would be appropriate. But no logic is powerful enough to sway me. I could not. I know why, in the instant of that realization, the totally natural life and death I preach is never going to happen completely. The human mind will never completely submit to cold reality.

CHAPTER 16

Confound Compound Interest: Our Almost Immortal Invention

I don't know if humankind tried to invent immortal money before or after Methuselah's day, but there is some archaeological evidence that, way back in prehistory, ancient Assyrians developed ways to buy stuff with no money down and no worry about how long it took to pay for. The idea did not get a firm hold on the more modern imagination, however, until the late Middle Ages, when the popes realized how much wealth they could manufacture by charging interest on money, something that earlier was punishable by excommunication. Up until then, the Christian religion (as well as Islam, and in fact all major religions as far as I can find) held that *all* interest on money was usury and therefore forbidden. In fact, almost everywhere that a garden or farm or pastoral economy held sway, interest on money was outlawed, which is why I am writing about it here. The fake immortality of interest on money is the enemy of the natural immortality of the food chain. After money interest became more or less legitimatized, great minds down through the centuries spent lots of energy uselessly arguing over how much interest was okay and how much was sinful. May the biggest bank win.

I grew up with a certain fondness for compound interest because it allowed me some ill-gained freedom when I was in grade school. (I swear the most important things in my life happened in my grade school years.) There was a boy, Ed, in my class for whom the notion of compounded money interest was most bewildering. I would like to argue, now, that he was the smartest one in our class because there is no rational meaning to money interest, and so a mind that by nature can't grasp the idea is the best of all minds in terms of innate intelligence. But in grade school I of course entertained no such deep thoughts. I only knew that the teacher, exasperated with Ed's inability to calculate compound interest, gave me the job of teaching him. I was to train him in how to become a successful banker. What made the job acceptable to me was that I was allowed to tutor Ed in the art of usury in the library, which was separate from the classrooms. There was no librarian present during the time I was to teach Ed, a big mistake any educator ought to know better than to make. Allow two boys the freedom of spending an unsupervised hour every school day and you can imagine what might happen. It was recess time for Ed and Gene. I really did try, at first, to show him how to figure 6 percent interest on a thousand dollars for a year, add on that amount to the original thousand, multiply it again, and again, and again, each "again" representing a year's time. In hardly fifty years a few bucks could magically grow its way into millions. It was not so much that Ed couldn't multiply. He didn't believe that he would ever have a thousand dollars that would grow to fifty thousand no matter what the numbers said. He didn't care, either, especially when there were other ways we could while away the time. Before long we were just talking or playing puzzle games and planning our escapades beyond the confines of school—our homes were just a mile apart across farm fields. The whole deal worked out well because the teacher could hardly hold me responsible when Ed continued to be mystified by usury. After all, she couldn't teach him, either.

Thinking back, I wonder if she was not the smartest teacher I ever had and understood how important it would be if she could get someone under her tutelage to understand the mighty, mischievous power of compound interest. Ed was not going to realize this perhaps, but maybe a quicker learner like me just might be capable of seeing deeper into the subject. The best way to learn anything is to try to teach it to someone else, and so she was hoping maybe that by attempting to teach Ed, I would come to realize the immortal possibilities of compound money interest. In that she was successful. I was well on the delusional road to becoming an investment banker. If I could somehow find a way to get a few thousand dollars in the bank and keep it there, I would die rich.

My parents had actually started me on this road even before this, literally praising me all the way to the bank where I proudly forked over my accumulated coins—a penny for every time I opened the barnyard gate for my grandfather and nickels and dimes my parents paid me for weeding the garden and cutting thistles out of the pasture field. The banker guy had this marvelous little machine into which he dumped my loose change, and, in a trice, it sorted out the coins into their various values, tabulated the total, whisked it away into the bank vault, and gave me in return a "bank book" in which my newly acquired wealth was recorded in total. I didn't need to have that sum recorded because it was already imprinted on my brain cells forever. But the bank book also told me that, at 3 percent interest, my $6.52 grew to $6.71 the first year. I would make almost two whole dimes for doing nothing—a sum that otherwise would come to me only by the laborious process of hoeing off two hundred bull thistles (two inches below ground level, and I better not cheat because my sister hoeing with me would squeal on me if I did) or opening the barnyard gate twenty times for grandfather. Wow.

If I had a million dollars in the bank, in the first year it would "earn" thirty thousand, an income that in 1937 was far beyond my imagination, and would increase faster and faster from then on. And there were people actually doing that! They lived in those big old mansions on South Sandusky Avenue in town. I did not yet realize that someone had to borrow that money and pay more interest on it than I was being paid for this magic to occur. I only knew that having a lot of money earning interest was the beginning of paradise on earth. I was an early acolyte at the altar of capitalism.

As my education continued, I learned that there was nothing in the whole wide world more hypocritical than the attitude of society toward interest on money. Although thoroughly denounced as usury by every wise philosopher and religious leader down through the ages, lending money on interest was everywhere practiced with gusto. It was just too neat a way to fuel economic growth, so I was taught. All those old curmudgeons who insisted it was also a neat way to fuel human greed just didn't understand progress.

I tried hard to understand economic growth. Money "grew" by multiplying percentages, but that was not what growth meant to a farm boy. Real stuff grew old and died. Old money just kept growing faster, summer and winter, night and day, second by second, a cash register that never stopped ringing up the bucks. Those sedate residents in the big old houses on the south side of town died, but their money never did. It just passed on to their heirs and kept on growing. All those lucky dogs had to do was to spend no more than the interest they were getting and they could play around at whatever activity pleased them without worrying if they ever made any money or not.

By then, as a young man, I realized that rich people's money did not "work" for them, did not "earn income" for them, but that this working and earning was done by the people who borrowed the money. My father was borrowing money so that he could expand his farming operation. He pointed out to me that there was a bit of madness involved because he had to pay 6 percent interest on his loan, which was about all that farming ever made in profit in his experience. Why was he doing it then? "We just gotta kinda stall around and hope farm prices go up," he answered. They did go up a little, but so did farming costs, of course, and then they went down again. *But the interest payments did not go down when the farm prices went down.* He never did get all of his "expansion debt" paid off until after his death when his farm was split up and sold. The debt never grew old and died like he did. I was surprised to find, about that time, that centuries ago Shakespeare had said it all: "Neither a borrower nor a lender be, for loan oft loses both itself and friend, and borrowing dulls the edge of husbandry."

I was even more surprised when teachers tried to instruct me about the Year of Jubilee in the Book of Leviticus in the Old Testament. The people back then supposedly practiced just what my father had needed. Every fifty years, in the Jubilee Year, all unpaid debts were forgiven. At least that was the way my teachers translated the biblical syntax, which I could rarely decipher. When I read Leviticus, or for that matter any book of the Old Testament, the text seemed so soaked in pronouns that I was never sure which one went to which antecedent. But one sentence in Leviticus seemed quite clear. Chapter 25, verse 28 reads: "But if his hands not find the means to repay the price, the buyer shall have what he bought until the year of the Jubilee. For in that year all that is sold shall return to the owner and to the ancient possessor." Or how about this, in verses 36 and 37: ". . . take not usury of him nor more than thou gavest . . . Thou shalt not give him thy money upon usury, nor exact of him any increase of fruits." When I asked what that meant exactly, teachers admitted that they were stumped by the "ancient possessor," too, but swore up and down that the Bible was the sacred word of God, and God was surely saying that debts should be forgiven every fifty years and charging interest on money was the sin of usury. Well, then, I countered, using our usual expression to begin a question: "'Hows come' nobody obeys God's sacred word?"

"Houses can't come," Father Hilary, our Bible history teacher would say primly. End of conversation. I asked a guy who owned a lot of bank shares about that one day. He stared at me and finally said that I was a danger to society. But I never forgot, like everyone else seemed to, this Jubilee Year thing and how it could have saved my father. If his land payments had been used to pay down the principal only, he would have been out of debt when he died.

So when I went out on my own, I was convinced that the only way to beat the world was to become a lender not a borrower, even if Shakespeare was against that, too. I did not join the consumer society. I did not buy anything unless I had to and then I bought cheap: cheap clothes, cheap house, cheap car, cheap everything. I borrowed for our first house and for one car and by living cheap we paid off both debts in double time and never borrowed money again. Not spending money did not oppress me. I was headed toward the kind of independence that Humphrey Bogart alluded to in an interview when he said that he did not care anything about money except that having it meant he could tell every son of a bitch who tried to boss him about what to do to go to hell. Many days I worked for minimum wages but worked nearly twice as many hours to make up the difference. That was the only way I could have afforded the life of an independent writer on a very moderate income. I even once or twice told an editor to go to hell. My real asset was a long-suffering wife who was willing to go along with such an impecunious lifestyle.

So finally I came to old age and the ultimate irony of the capitalistic superstition about money growth. By dint of very careful parsimony we did save enough money to provide for our retirement, along with Social Security. Then the pseudo-capitalists, after exhorting me to save money all those years so they could lend it out, decreed that our savings would no longer earn any interest. The Federal Reserve said it had to do this "to boost the economy." In other words, the way to keep the Federal Reserve's reserves growing was to make sure mine didn't. I had finally learned what

I had suspected all the time. The Bible and all those wise philosophers had it right for once: Interest on money was at the root of our social problems.

I complained to a good friend who farms about five hundred acres of corn and soybeans. He was also complaining because he had been farming over a thousand acres but lost out to larger farms willing to pay more to rent or buy land. As we stared at each other, his thoughts took a turn I'd never heard from him before.

"Why do we need money at all?" he asked.

I looked at him as if he were losing his mind. He had always seemed to be a very practical, no-nonsense, non-whimsical kind of guy. He answered his own question.

"We don't really, you know. We really don't. Everything that money can buy, that we really need to survive happily, is right here in front of us. The land. The food it grows. The doctors who can operate on us. The medicine we need. The police. The cars. The houses and housing materials. Everything is right here, staring us in the face. But suddenly we say we can't have it without money, as if without money the life support system wouldn't exist. If we just went on doing what we do, we could just trade around our services and all would be fine."

"You assume that everyone loves what they do whether they get paid or not."

"I keep on farming even when there's no money in it for me. You say yourself that you keep writing even though you could make a lot more money doing something else. You say you don't care about the money. Neither do I. Maybe everyone feels that way."

"Except that without money, you'd have to quit farming and let the big guys take your land away from you."

"Yes, but if there wasn't any money, the big guys wouldn't do that. Would they?"

"Who are you going to get to do the dirty work like cleaning windows on high-rises and repairing broken gutters and working on assembly lines?" To me factory work was the bottom of the pit.

"Hey, lots of people like factory work. I bet a good window washer likes what he does."

"Even if he doesn't get paid well?"

"Hey, I know guys who say they wouldn't sit at a computer writing all day no matter how much you paid 'em. They think you're nuts."

"Well, I think I'm nuts, too. But that's not the point. People are all imperfect. You have to fool them with money to make them work."

"I'm not so sure."

I turned off the conversation. I was too overwhelmed by the fact that this practical, everyday sort of guy, whose world was surrounded by hundred-thousand-dollar machines and barns full of cow manure, who despised classrooms and barely endured them through high school, could have such lofty thoughts. If humans were rational, as we insisted we were, why indeed did we need money? A world without money would surely be heaven on earth.

Not getting interest on our money did not really put us in dire straits, as I soon learned. We could cope with the lack of planned-for retirement income the way we had always coped. We had learned to be content and happy enough on a small income, so we merely had to continue to live as we had always lived and keep on working as long as we were physically able, which is what we wanted to do anyway.

My education was complete. Actually it was complete many years ago when my grandfather told me—and I tell my grandchildren every chance I get—that in the runaway inflation of Germany in the early 1920s (which is the disease that compound interest on money contracts right before it finally does die), the rich people traded their gems and jewels to the peasants for potatoes. Grandfather knew because some of those peasants were our ancestors. Potatoes are a whole lot more immortal than money.

----------◆----------

CHAPTER 17

How to Survive People

*A*s I rested between bouts of splitting firewood, I noticed that sweat bees were clustering on the maul like they usually do on my arms if I let them. Hmmm. I should have figured it out right away. They were licking at the salt on the maul handle that my perspiration had left there. I rested a little longer than I normally would, thinking about how nature adapts so well to its most dangerous and unpredictable member—the human being. Sweat bees of course don't think they are adapting to anything. It is just business as usual for them. They will take a little salt wherever they can find it, not wondering, as humans would be prone to do, about why some all-powerful God had been so kind as to provide them with this unanticipated beneficence. Nor would they worry that since maul handles aren't a customary source of their food, maybe this kind of salt wasn't good for them.

Nor did the opossums that once wintered in our grain combine bother themselves with any such lofty notions of cause and effect.

To them my Allis-Chalmers All-Crop was just another hollow tree, albeit one with an uncommonly large hole in it. The feral cat that decided to raise her kittens in the same machine showed a bit more imagination in the art of adaptability. She snuggled her young into the bottom of the auger spout in the empty grain bin where she could pounce on a mouse now and then that came looking for stray grains of wheat left over from harvest time. Imagine the kittens' surprise, to say nothing of my own, when I revved up the combine in June, in preparation for another season of harvesting, and out of the auger tumbled three very frightened mouse lovers. They were not even injured. And speaking of mice, there is something about the battery compartment of my old John Deere tractor that they can't resist. Every month or so, there will be a new nest right on top of the battery. (A mechanic told me that those Bounce napkins you put in the clothes dryer have an odor that deters mice from chewing battery wires.) The nest itself is the epitome of adaptability—frizzly stuff the mice scavenged from old grain sacks, disintegrating rags, paper, globs of wool left over from shearing, and corn silk from husked ears of corn. I do not speak mouse language so I can't say what they find so irresistible about the tractor. Possibly they know that inside the compartment they are safe from cats.

Birds are even more adaptable. The robins play blissfully in the water from the garden sprinkler. A recent news report tells of birds using cigarette butts in nest building. Our birds pull strands of plastic from the frayed tarps we use to cover haystacks. Bluebirds seem to stick around all winter now. They feast on our red cedar berries, even come to our front door to eat the berries on the Christmas wreath that Carol hangs there. Neither red cedar nor multiflora rose is native here, but their arrival seems to correspond with the time bluebirds started staying all winter. Where our daughter and son-in-law planted Bradford pears around their patio, the bluebirds clustered in flocks on the dried fruit in late winter. One year a pair of indigo buntings built their nest in the thick leafy vines of our pole beans growing up a trellis. A robin once built her nest on the upright end of the sickle bar mower when it was parked in the shed. A phoebe persists in building a nest on the curved section of a downspout on the house roof. Another builds her nest on a joist in the barn just three feet above my head. Barn swallows of course have gotten their name by using barn beams for their homes, almost always anchoring the nest on an electric light fixture if one is available. In a parking lot early one morning, I noticed several crows cawing while perched on a sign that directed shoppers where to leave shopping carts. But the crows were not there to draw my attention to the sign. They were flying from one bit of papery trash blowing across the blacktop to another, examining then for scraps of food left by human litterers.

So well have animals taken to modern farm machinery that mouse and bird nests have become a major source of fires in tractors and combines. These giant, complex machines depend on an intricate network of electrical wiring running hither and yon through them. Where the wires congregate, deep in a machine's bowels, birds seem to see some sort of similarity to a webwork of vines or twigs and build nests there. The wires get hot and worn or chewed by mice and then sometimes a stray spark results. Like tinder, the nest goes up in flames, and then the combine. It happened to a neighbor. He says that some makes and models of grain harvesters seem more attractive to the birds than others. I shall not name names here, since that preference might be just a matter of chance, and I surely don't want any particular manufacturer to think I have a personal vendetta against its machines. I have a personal vendetta against *all* monster machines.

Bats love our barn. To them it is another cave. When we built it, we joined the rafters where they meet at the apex of the roof with plywood plates on both sides of the two-by-sixes. The space enclosed was, unbeknownst to us, just what bats like for habitation and co-habitation. About half of those twenty unplanned bat houses are occupied every summer, and we have few mosquitoes around the barn even though it sits in the woods. The bats have a steady supply of food because the barrel that catches water from the roof is almost always wiggling with mosquito larvae. The mosquitoes of course are also adapting to human civilization by taking advantage of the barrel, while the bats take advantage of us and the mosquitoes.

Those of us with strong environmental leanings tend to despair over human activity that seems to be, or actually is, destructive to the rest of nature (and eventually ourselves). From the standpoint of searching for the meaning of eternal life, I think we often overdo our worries and need to take a longer look at how often human endeavors, even the most selfish—especially the most selfish—play themselves out in the face of patient nature. Contemplate the lowly but everlasting jellyfish mentioned in chapter 12. Perhaps if we weren't so intelligent, or would quit thinking futilely about life after death, we could learn to become biologically immortal, too. Our religious theologians want us to believe that their gods govern a universe beyond our control, and our economic theologians teach us that money is the god that controls everything whether we like it or not. We are supposed to bow down and adore in either case. I think we should try to mimic nature more instead. The sweat bee does not fold its little wings akimbo and declare that it never has sucked maul handles before and is not, by God, about to start now. It just licks. If nothing bad happens, it goes on licking. We should think about reacting to our own foibles and greed in a similar fashion. I often think about what a missionary in Africa once told me: "There is no such thing as a trash problem here. If you dump a load of typical American junk along the road in Africa, it will be all gone by morning. The natives will find a use for every bit of it."

A recent book, *Nature Wars*, discusses a good example of how to survive people. The subtitle says it all: *The Incredible Story of How Wildlife Comebacks Turned Backyards into Battlegrounds* (by Jim Sterba, Crown Publishers, 2012). Fifty years ago, we worried that many species of wildlife were headed for extinction. Today many of these species have increased to where wildlife control is a lucrative new career. Fifty years ago, the experts said that small contrary farmers were headed for extinction, too. Now the countryside and urban backyards are full of them.

Another good example of nature surviving people is our highway system. From an environmental point of view, all those roads pose danger to nature. But there is collateral advantage as well as collateral damage. Those thousands of deer–car collisions, killing both deer and humans, at least alleviate the overpopulation of deer. (I dare not, of course, suggest that highways reduce the overpopulation of humans, too.) Even roadkill benefits nature. As you drive along, note how many hawks, buzzards, and eagles are perched along the highways waiting for cars to kill more furry little animals for them to eat. If it were not for traffic, raccoons by now would surely have upset the precarious balance of nature because of their destructiveness (their ability to adapt to humans), and even the Humane Society would be calling for their blood.

While one is tempted to bemoan all that land covered with concrete and asphalt roadways, it means thousands upon thousands of acres alongside the roads festooned with plants of all kinds, providing a lot of carbon sequestration and a mecca for insects and birds. Also thousands upon thousands of new ponds have been created along the highways to provide fill dirt for the highway beds. We are quick to mourn the number of migrating birds killed by high-tension wires and tall buildings, and rightly so. But why not rejoice in the countervailing good effect of human activity, in this case highways, on wildlife, on water levels in the soil, perhaps even on weather itself, all of which comes from all those roadside ponds and lakes?

I do not wish with these examples to underplay the environmental damage that's going on, but just to suggest that nature is a whole lot tougher than we appreciate. Where degradation is in progress, as in mountaintop removal of coal, or soil erosion from too much cultivation, nature will eventually have the last word.

Money greed will, in the long run, cause its own collapse. At least looking at the degradation with a bit of hopefulness might lower your blood pressure, another step toward extending one's personal mortality, if not immortality. Instead of slamming large-scale farming (as I so often do), why not contemplate what is happening despite it? Yes, thousands of acres are going to monocultured corn and soybeans, with concomitant soil degradation and the consolidation of landownership in fewer and fewer hands. Yet nature, silently and patiently, is showing us how to adapt to it, endure it, and overcome it. For one thing, all that corn fodder—stalks and leaves and roots generated by all the fertilizer—goes mostly back into the soil to build organic matter. All those year-round wet holes that are increasing in size in many cultivated fields, despite all that technology can invent to stop them, are good for frogs and water birds and insects of all kinds. We have flocks of gulls around in the spring now that were rare in earlier times. The wet holes also retain moisture for drought times. As already has happened in some instances, the farmers have to give up destructive commercial grain practices in these areas, and nature slowly, silently, takes them over. Nearly every day I pass badly eroded hillsides abandoned for farming that are now growing slowly back into woodland.

The "get big or get out" mentality that affects large-scale farming has other beneficial side effects. Getting big can also become a ticket to getting out. Big farming can't profitably farm small creekside hills and ravines, as I pointed out in the first chapter. So these little patches of land are turning into wildlife sanctuaries. Wild animals use them as refuges and foray into the immensity of the grain fields around them to eat. Deer in Ohio are fatter and larger than deer in Wyoming. Also, the farmers who engineer what look like gigantic monocultures of cotton and grain are as human and loving of nature as the rest of us in many ways. They build farm ponds that dot the farmland in ever-increasing numbers. These ponds, along with the highway ponds, are one reason why the American eagle, which prefers fish to lambs for food, is increasing in numbers here in the Midwest, the last place one might have thought, a few years ago, that they would proliferate.

The number of fish in these ponds is increasing dramatically. As far as I can find out, no one has any clear notion of just how much. We are too intent on accentuating the negative, like how Asian carp are invading our waterways. Asian carp, by the way, make a good example of how we can mimic nature's adaptability. There are efforts now to make this fish a delicacy in fancy restaurants.

There are many more ways we can adapt. For example, instead of using up our energies harping about big farmers (whom of course we need right now to provide enough food for all of us), buy your own little patch of land to turn into an oasis of food and wildlife abundance. More and more people are doing this rather than standing around wringing their hands about global warming. Your little sanctuary will not be prone to disappear when the inevitable financial crises hit the big commercial farms. Second, instead of ranting about the overpopulation of deer (which I do often), shoot a couple every season and provide your family with a year's supply of meat. Deer tags do not cost as much as the venison is worth as food. Think about it this way. You are outwitting the new American oligarchy. You are getting your meat almost free while not aiding and abetting the corn, soybean, and animal factory plutocracy.

Start a garden farm right there on the maul handle of large-scale industrial grain land. You don't need a big patch to do it, or a rural area for that matter. A tenth of an acre in town can make an unbelievably fruitful little paradise complete with pond, greenhouse, and even a few chickens.

Buy a patch of land with trees on it for your own refuge as well as wildlife's and to provide your own home heat. If that's out of your reach, physically or economically, buy a couple of bare acres and start a grove on it just for fun. Or turn your backyard into a grove. Watching trees grow is as rewarding as gardening. Actually if you just set aside the land from all development, nature will adapt it into woodland or prairie or desert, depending on your climate. There are no such things as vacant lots or abandoned farms. Nature will always fill them with life. You can then watch a very interesting live documentary about natural adaptation, one that changes every month and every year.

I wonder at how many more bluebirds there are now compared with when I was a child, simply because building bluebird houses has become a fashionable thing to do. I wonder how much the songbird population has increased in general because so many people are feeding birds in their backyards. Maybe the increase due to human help equals or exceeds the decrease from destructive human activity. Yes, birds do fly into our obscenely tall buildings, but remember, too, those hawks and owls and chimney swifts that have adapted to our architectural monstrosities. I have a notion there is about as much wildlife in cities now as in an equal amount of rural land outside them. Detroit has plenty of empty, crumbling buildings perfect for wildlife habitation. That city is already mimicking the adaptability of nature. A farm of several hundred acres is being established in a part of the city lost to residential and business development.

If you begin to get pleasure out of finding environmentally friendly niches and cracks and crannies in the seeming dreadnought of human advances against nature, you will also find yourself achieving some of the patience and tranquility that nature shows in the face of adversity. The medical profession can almost guarantee you that you will be rewarded with a longer mortal life, and it surely won't shorten your immortal life one second.

————◆————

CHAPTER 18

Staying Longer
in the Saddle

*O*bviously the first step down the path toward immortality
is to put off mortality as long as possible. For the aging
but active person, especially around the garden farm,
that should mean, as a guiding principle, to resolve not to do today
what you can put off until tomorrow. This not only will keep you
alive longer, but will often result in greater efficiency. For example,
last summer a nice stand of lamb's-quarter grew up around the
chicken coop. Every time I decided to cut it down—"neatin' up
the barnyard," as we farmers are inclined to say—they had grown
another six inches, and I finally became intrigued with just how
tall this weed could grow. Or so I rationalized my laziness. Well.
They grew as tall as the coop, eight feet high. I did a little research.
I could find no specific reference as to lamb's-quarter's limits to
growth, but did learn that the leaves make good salad and excellent
forage for livestock, and the seeds are more nutritious than farm

grains. Birds of all kinds eat them. That would include chickens. I decided not to "neatin' up" anymore, no matter what visitors would think. When anyone chided me for not keeping the hen lot as straight and tidy as a Prussian army outpost, I would arch my brow piously and say that the trashy weeds made shade for the hens in the hot weather, and shielded them from hawks.

When the lamb's-quarter seed matured, I could not tell for sure if the hens were eating it, although they showed little interest in the corn I was also feeding them. When winter came, the seeds scattered on top of the snow. A flock of juncos took up residence and ate them. I presume other birds did also. Eventually the stalks fell over and mostly disappeared under the snow. Next spring the area around the chicken coop looked almost as if I had kept it mowed the whole preceding summer. This is what happens when one inculcates within his soul the virtue of laziness.

I doubt that farming success has ever been achieved without a grim, gritty resolve to accept sweat, pain, long hours, and nose-to-the-grindstone dedication, so I don't want to deprecate the notion of *no pain, no gain*. After such a lifetime, the aging farmer or gardener has developed a reflex habit of bending eagerly to every task at hand, and considers slowing down or outright loafing as a sign of weakness of character. Instead of coasting a bit into old age, successful people want to keep right on forging stalwartly ahead with little regard for their bodies. Not smart. Early to bed and early to rise may make a man healthy, wealthy, and wise, but it can also mean early to bed in a hospital where early to rise isn't going to happen.

To survive in the front lines, the wise farmer or gardener must develop a fast track to the hammock and a studied slowness with the hayfork and the hoe. Sometimes the phrase *work ethic* is an oxymoron. It may be noble to get two blades of grass to grow where only one grew before, but sometimes one is enough.

Patience is so often a key to the secrets of immortality. I ended up once in the hospital with a hernia because of impatience with "dumb animals," who in fact are a whole lot smarter than they seem to be. I was trying to drive a few ewes across the creek. They were not quite ready to go wading. They wanted to ponder alternatives. I grabbed one of them and literally threw her across the water. I could almost feel my gut ripping apart.

Wisdom of a sort came to me in time. One must allow sheep to make up their own minds. I learned to coax them slowly and gradually down close to the creek bank, then sit down on a log and contemplate the universe. I am almost sure that the sheep knew I wanted them to cross the shallow, narrow strip of water, but they wanted it to be their idea, not mine. I think it must have taken them half an hour to make up their minds and cross the creek, but half an hour spent sitting on a log watching the birds was a whole lot better than lying in bed for three days watching hospital walls.

Sometimes I have to follow that contemplative approach to life just to get them to go into the barn. It is really easy once you understand the minds of sheep. First put hay in their feed racks in the barn. Close the lot gate. Go to the house and eat lunch or something. Eventually the sheep decide it is time to go in the barn and in they go. Come back later and quietly slip around to the barn door and close the sheep in. It is so easy, but so hard for a stubborn human who thinks he must get animals to follow his schedule, not theirs.

Another example: Last year, with a very wet spring, I could not get my pastures mowed until the fescue had grown up belt-high and so thick my old rotary mower would barely chew through the jungle. I was quite distraught. I am first of all not a fan of fescue, even though it does make tolerable winter grazing. I thought I needed to mow the stuff before it went to seed or it would take over the more desirable bluegrass and clover. Now I could not mow. Then the driest summer in years set in. All the pastures stopped growing. Was I going to have to feed hay in the summer? But I noticed that the sheep were wading through the tall fescue and nibbling at the seedheads. Hmmm. Research (asking around) revealed that, yes, they would eat fescue seeds. And that is exactly what they did all through July and August, along with the coarse fescue stems and what little clover and other grasses they could find. I did not have to feed any hay. September arrived, and with it rain. And more rain in October. The old tall fescue stems, or what remained of them, broke over, and from the ground sprang a vigorous growth of bluegrass along with some new fescue and some clover. By November I had a beautiful pasture, almost as if I had kept the fields mowed all summer. Through no fault of my own, I had saved not only the work of mowing, but a lot of fuel and wear and tear on the mower. All the past years, I had been mowing more than I needed to just to make the pastures look neat and golf-coursey.

I like to argue that the glorification of neatness has caused more injuries and deaths on the farm than laziness. I think of a farmer in our community who in old age kept on mowing ungrazed hillsides and vales like all of us old farmers love to do. He had finally sold his animals, but still kept mowing just for neatness' sake. Every weed had to be clipped, even in the more inaccessible places on the farm. One day he went after that very last clump of grass that had marred his vision of perfection along the creek, and in the process the tractor tipped over the creek bank and he was killed.

A close friend narrowly escaped the same fate on a steep hill.

"Why are you mowing that hill?" I asked him.

"Gotta keep the brush from growing up."

"Why?"

"Well, it will ruin the pasture."

"But you don't use it for pasture anymore anyway. You don't have any livestock and don't plan to have any."

"Well, it just looks awful growing up in thorns."

"You know as well as I do that there are little trees growing up in there, too. Eventually they will take over."

"Yes, but right now it looks like I'm a lazy, trashy farmer."

I rest my case.

Another tendency of the workaholic is to follow the rule that says if a little is good, more is better. I dare not name names, but here are a few case histories.

a. Two newcomers to the local food movement decided they wanted their own eggs. They built a bit of a coop in the backyard and put six hens in it. Everything worked out fine. So they got forty hens. They did not have land enough for that many, did not have food for that many, did not have time to sell the eggs of that many, and, most of all, did not have bedding for the manure of that many. They had to build a bigger coop, had to start buying feed and straw, and if they were going to get commercially serious about selling eggs, needed more hens. Neighbors started complaining about odor and flies, real or imagined. The backyard pioneers became discouraged, got rid of their chickens, and ever after told everyone that "there's no money" in eggs.

b. An ambitious gardener got enamored of mulch gardening. He asked me to come and give him some advice. I found him in the middle of about an acre of garden, part of it mulched with about a foot of old hay. Three of his children were standing around, wielding forks. From the looks on their faces, they were by no means happy. I did not know what to say. I didn't want to discourage this guy, but trying to mulch that much garden was a beastly task, and it was actually too early in the year, in my estimation, to put down thick mulch. The ground hadn't warmed up enough yet. I mumbled something to that effect and said something cautionary about the weed seeds that his spoiled hay mulch probably harbored. But I tried to show admiration for his zeal in raising his own food, even though I had a strong hunch this endeavor was headed for failure simply because it was too much, too fast. In August I drove by the place to see a jungle of high weeds and no garden. P.S. This man quit "gardening," saying he did not have time for it, and none of his children ever touched a hoe or a fork again as far as I know.

c. A husband and wife moved to the country to live the good life. She was quite apprehensive about the whole idea, something he admitted after their divorce. He put out big patches of peas, beans, and corn the first year, "getting his feet wet" as he said, with a dream of making a living in the market farm business someday. Unfortunately, or maybe fortunately, he had to keep his other job, which required traveling and being away from home during the week sometimes. "I had to take care of all that garden and then harvest and process it almost all by myself," his wife said. "It was downright slavery."

d. An erstwhile new farmer, full of admirable ambition, bought a place in the country and invested in small numbers of livestock. Again, he had an outside job that kept him on the road much of the time. Sure enough, the cows and horses kept getting out and his poor wife, usually trailing two squalling children, had to try to get the animals back inside the broken-down fences. This was a classic case of putting the cart before the horse, or rather the horse before good fencing.

Most often, mortality in farming and gardening ventures stems from an overabundance of eager vigor not balanced by savvy muscles. Around the age of forty, people—especially men who have long yearned to be farmers—get their chance. They have enough money, enough time, enough know-how, and enough energy to make it work. Usually, they have another career or job, so they end up working very long hours on and off the homestead, all hours of the day and night, all weekend long. They don't mind because they love working on their little farm paradises. I have watched people I know and admire very much go this route, and on one occasion I even told a friend that he was going to hurt himself because his enthusiasm was in much better shape than his muscles. He just laughed. But then his back gave out on him and he had to quit long before he wanted to. But that was better than a heart attack, which is usually the way these sad stories end.

Newcomers to the farming and gardening way of life often do not come from backgrounds where they experience a lot of physical work as they grow up. (As a grade schooler, I had to shovel wagon-loads of wheat, oats, and corn into bins and cribs during harvest. I had to learn how to handle a scoop shovel for hours at a time, or die.) They go at it in middle age with great zest, but ignorance about the basic tricks of using body leverage to save backs, spines, legs, intestines, and muscles. On a farm, there is always something heavy that needs to be moved, and the uninitiated do not realize that in many of these cases, the lever and the fulcrum that make easier work of the lifting can be parts of the human body itself. It is easy enough to bend over, pick up a bale of hay by the strings, and sling it three tiers up in the barn. Hey, look how strong I am. But that kind of strength does not go far into the day, and for an older person not accustomed to or conditioned to heavy physical work, it can spell disaster. Veterans of the hay fields know that knees, hips, backbones, and shoulders are the levers and fulcrums that, when used properly to buck bales, make the work easier and less damaging to the body. For example, the veteran hay bale handler will always use a hay hook to lift bales if he is going to be working at it for long periods of time, especially if the bales weigh more than sixty or seventy pounds. He will set the hook into the bale close to one end, then tip it up on the other end but without ever lifting the whole weight of the bale. Then he will reset the hook down about three-fourths of the way toward the other end as the bale stands on end. Next—and this is the part that doesn't show—he will sidle his body up against the standing bale and put his knee against it about halfway down on the opposite side of the hook. As he lifts the bale with the hook and one arm, he pushes his knee against the bale on the other side. The knee—along with his hip, which is also against the bale—acts as a fulcrum, taking some of the weight of the bale off his arm and, more important, off his back as he lifts it. The momentum that moves the bale through the air then helps send it into its final resting place onto the stack of bales. When you get good at it, you can sock that bale exactly where you want it in the stack without having to shift or wiggle it around, again saving back and arms.

Forking manure is also a matter of using the body along with the fork, as a lever and fulcrum. If you just thrust the fork into the manure bedding trampled solid by the animals and try to lift it straight up, your back will sooner or later give out, and usually sooner. You must at all times try to protect your muscles and joints from bearing the full weight of whatever you are moving. First of all, slide the fork under only about four inches of layered manure. Then push down on the handle (the lever in this action). The curve in the fork tines becomes a fulcrum, and the forkful of manure is thus loosened from the bedding. Sometimes, after you push down on your lever-handle, you must then lift the handle up and forward a little to break loose the manure on your fork from the bedding. In this maneuver, the pointed ends of the tines become the fulcrum for the handle-lever. After loosening the manure, you lift with both hands. When the forkful comes clear of the bedding, the hand that is halfway down the fork handle becomes the fulcrum as you steady the load in the air, lift it with both arms sharing the weight, and swing the whole of it over to the spreader. The momentum created helps carry the forkful through the air. Then you turn over the fork above the spreader, your hand in the middle of the handle still acting as a sort of fulcrum and the handle above it, guided by your other hand, still the lever as you plop the manure into the spreader. In the whole operation, no one part of the body, especially not the back or legs, ever bears the brunt of the full weight of the forkful of manure.

Lever wisdom can add strength to muscles as age weakens those of us who persist in staying in the saddle longer than we probably should. If a rusty burr and bolt refuse to budge even after being soaked in Liquid Wrench and rapped with a hammer, slide a length of two-inch pipe over the wrench handle, giving the wrench more leverage, and try again. This can be dangerous. If you use too long a piece of pipe, you can generate enough leverage to break the wrench rather than loosen the bolt. But with a little common sense and what amounts to gentleness now that you have a sizable lever, you can usually turn the rusty burr on the bolt, not wreck the wrench.

Another common predicament for old farmers is pulling out fence posts. Nowadays, nearly everyone has a tractor with a hydraulic bucket, which can save many a back. Wrap a log chain around the post, hook it to the bucket, raise the bucket, and ease the post out of the ground. But there is a very old-fashioned way to do the same thing, if you farm with horses or a tractor without hydraulic lift. Lean a two-by-six of very strong wood—like oak— against the post to be pulled about three-quarters of the way up. (Weaker wood will likely split.) Cut a slight notch in the top end of that board. Run a log chain from around the bottom of the post at ground level and then up and over the edge of the board leaning against the post and then on out to your tractor's drawbar or your horse's whippletree. As the tractor or horses ease into the pull, the board forces the chain to pull upward from the bottom of the post and the post loosens and comes up at least most of the way out of the ground as the board is pulled to a vertical position.

The hand-cranked windlass and the winch were much more common around the farm in pre-hydraulic times. Essentially both are drums turned by cranks and equipped with a rope or chain to move or lift much more than mere muscle power can do. When powered by small motors, winches are quite powerful.

All rope-and-pulley arrangements use the winch and windlass technology to some extent. I use my block and tackle often in situations where the tractor and hydraulic bucket aren't practical. For example, to make sure a tree I am cutting down falls where I want it to fall, that's the tool to use, because if the tree falls on the rope nothing is harmed compared with the tree falling on the tractor.

One of the old-time uses of winching or windlass power is still handy to know about today if forestry and woodcutting are part of your homesteading life. A fairly large log can be rolled onto a wagon or flatbed truck with a small tractor or team of horses by rolling it up stout boards slanted from the ground to the wagon or truck bed. Two ropes are attached to the vehicle and run underneath the log positioned parallel to the vehicle and then back to the tractor or horses on the other side of the vehicle. As the ropes are pulled in unison, they roll the log up the slanted loading boards and onto the truck or wagon bed. The full weight of the log is borne by the earth and the loading boards, not the tractor or horses.

I use this method often to move small to medium-sized logs by hand. I lay out two tracks made of saplings about three feet apart (think railroad track), and jockey the log I want to move onto these "tracks" with a peavey or cant hook. Even an old man can still feel strong with a peavey in his hands. Once on its wooden tracks, a log of quite hefty size can be rolled along, again using the peavey. If the log is lying at right angles to the direction you want to roll it, use the peavey to edge it up onto one piece of wood under the middle of the log. Then it is easy to swivel it around in the direction you want to roll it. Needless to say, being able to move such weighty objects with puny muscle power dramatically increases your sense of superiority.

Even small buildings can be moved this way. Once I wanted to move a little chicken coop several hundred feet. The direction was downhill and I had lots of manpower available—this was in the seminary, where we were supposed to be studying Holy Scripture, not egg production. We nailed two-by-eight runners at the bottom of both long sides of the coop and laid out two tracks (again, think railroad tracks) downhill toward the coop's new destination. We had a few nice round posts, which, when placed between the runners and the track, gave the coop exceedingly great mobility. Once we pried the coop into motion, it moved right along on the rolling posts more miraculously than anything in Holy Scripture.

The only thing that saved us was that the coop would run out of rollers or track and skid to a stop until we jacked it up and added more roller and track from behind the coop. So by fits and starts we made it to the bottom of the hill. There was nothing so awesome as watching the coop at full speed right before running out of rollers as it rumbled downhill. If we had laid out track down the entire hillside, the coop would surely have been going fast enough to juggernaut into the house on the other side of our property line.

Once I had some eight-foot logs of about fourteen inches in diameter and only a pickup truck to do the hauling. How was I going to load them, since at the time I had no tractor with a hydraulic bucket on the front? What I did have was a wooden beam about fifteen feet long by three inches thick. I drilled a hole in it at mid-length. A heavy bolt through the hole and through a makeshift stand (fulcrum) about four feet high provided me with a huge lever. I chained one end of the lever to a log and then, pulling down on the other end, I could raise one end of the log just high enough to back the pickup under it. My poor wife or son operated the pickup during these maneuvers. Then I loosened the chain and reattached it to the other end of the log, still on the ground, and bore down on my giant lever again. A little more backing of the truck and the log was loaded. I was so proud of myself. I called my giant lever "Hercules."

A toboggan and a little snow is an easy way to get a bale of hay out to winter pasture. It is nice and low to the ground and you can roll a bale on it without much wear and tear on your back. Snow with a little ice is even better, dangerously better. One such wintry day, I had to contend with a dead ewe (sheep just love to die) lying unsightly behind the barn. I didn't want to crank up the tractor in such weather. My grandson and I were on our way to the hills next to the creek for some tobogganing. The fields back to the creek are all downhill, gently, and then rather steeply where the sledding hills slope to the creek. That ewe must have weighed over 250 pounds, but it skidded right along on the ice. When we reached the brim of the steeper hillside, Evan and I looked at each other and nodded. Yes. We straddled the dead ewe and took off. Not in the annals of shepherding history has a dead sheep ever moved so fast. The fence along the creek loomed up ahead of us. It was either bail out or maybe die. The toboggan and its dead copilot continued on, at a speed upwards of thirty miles an hour, I bet. The toboggan stopped when it hit the fence but its rider never paused, flattening the fence, hurtling onward until a tree stopped it. If it wasn't dead before, it surely was now.

To stay active in farm work well into old age, do not shun mechanical aids, as I did at first. I despised four-wheelers roaring over the farmland, disturbing my peace and quiet. Until our grandsons overruled me, I prohibited them from our farm. Came a day when getting around the fields, even getting back to the barn, was a trial. So I bought one of the rip-roarers. Smartest move I ever made, even if I can't hear the birds when I'm riding on it.

I was about to say the same for garden tillers, but I've learned something odd in this regard. For actual tilling or plowing—that is, turning the soil over and burying sod growth—the tiller beats the spade. But for cultivating I've learned, to my surprise, that hoeing maybe twenty minutes every day is actually easier on my body than moving the tiller around in confined garden rows and trying to do the whole garden at once. The secret is to have a sharp hoe, with the blade at just the right angle to the handle so that it hits the ground almost horizontally when you swing it into action. Old hoes are invariably designed better than new ones, and sometimes you can buy them cheap at farm auctions. Keep the hoe close to the ground and use short strokes. When you see someone raising the hoe over their head and slamming it to the ground, you can bet they will soon be in the market for a mechanical tiller.

Today there are warehouses full of labor-savers, most of which I ridiculed in my younger days. Mechanical posthole diggers and post pounders are kind of nice when you get past seventy, although I have managed to avoid them so far. I wait slyly for my stalwart son or grandson to pull in the driveway and then hand them the hand digger. Leaf blowers I still consign to the regions of the cuckoo's nest, but I am ready for a mower attachment that sucks up clipped grass and leaves in bags. If I were richer and just starting out, I'd have heated sidewalks and driveway, too. There is nothing more pathetic than old neatniks out there frantically shoveling snow until they keel over with a heart attack. Snowblowers are a little better, but you can get a heart attack trying to start the blamed things on a cold morning. Most of the time, in most of the United States, the snow will melt if you wait a day or two. When one must get out, old people become very adept at easing the car out a driveway covered with six inches of snow. It requires an extremely delicate foot on the accelerator. Snow tires can handle shallow snow, and the second time over goes easier. The possibility for immortality is greatly enhanced with four-wheel drive. If you think you can't afford that, keep a couple hundred pounds of ballast in the trunk and work on your foot–accelerator relationship. Better yet, at least for retirees, stay home until the weather clears.

---◆---

CHAPTER 19

Secret Crying Places

*T*he morning after grandson Evan scored the winning basket at the sound of the buzzer in a local high school game, I was up in the haymow as usual, throwing down hay for the sheep. I happened to look over in the corner of the loft and there lay, forgotten, a basketball, half deflated now, close by the old banking board and hoop, cobwebs dangling from them. No telling how many hours over the last decade Grandmother and I played here with our grandsons, Evan and Alex. I stared at the crumpled ball and wondered if maybe, just maybe, all those years of passing, dribbling, and shooting there in the barn were the reason Evan made that last desperate four-second drive to the basket and won the game. And yes, I was crying my eyes out.

The barn was a fitting enough place for tears, one of my secret "crying places" where no one was going to hear or see me. Over the years I have gone there regularly to mark the passage of time. The crying is hard to explain because I am usually remembering something that was not really sad, like when our son and daughter left home to make their own homes, as they should do. I cried, I think, because the passage of time marks the death of a boy or girl becoming a teenager or a teenager moving on to manhood or womanhood. These kinds of death are really more final than a body becoming a corpse. A corpse decomposes and returns to life. Days of boyhood never come back.

I doubt I would write about secret crying places except that I have learned how many other people have such hideouts, too. We have to cry unseen. Must never let the young ones know. Must never reveal our emotions. Would make the children feel bad.

As the years pass, it becomes harder to keep the tears back. An old song might bring them on, without any warning. Yesteryear's photographs almost always do. I first started needing a secret crying place when my mother died, fairly young. We were living in the suburbs of Philadelphia then, but I had still managed to make a secluded place in our backyard that seemed far from the madding crowd. At the very center of this secret garden was a rather ramshackle chicken coop I had put together with free construction materials. I could sit inside it on an overturned bucket, hidden from view except for the chickens querulously eyeing me with heads cocked sideways, as only chickens can do. I would remember my mother who was always singing and cry myself back from the grave. Sometimes the chickens would join me, although I knew they were singing, not weeping. Their singing helped.

I found more need for secret crying places when my grandsons were barely boys. We had walked across the pasture, as we did nearly every day for awhile there, and this time we strolled past what I called the boneyard, where I left dead sheep for the buzzards to eat. There were two sheep skeletons there that day, and they arrested the boys' attention.

"What does it mean to be dead?" Alex asked. He was down on his knees, staring at the skulls. He was hardly four years old, and I was startled at his question. What could I say?

"You are looking at deadness," I said bluntly. It just came out that way.

Silence. I was mortified: such a young boy, having to deal with the concept of death. But he said nothing, just looked queerly at the bones, then stood up and walked away, his usual joyous manner repressed for the moment.

As a boy myself, I became sort of numb to death. One of the cruelties worked upon me and classmates in grade school was being obliged to sing in the school choir for funerals. Catholic funerals in those days were wrapped in Latin dirges of sonorous Gregorian chant, enough in themselves to bring tears to the eyes. Attending funerals regularly that way, I became totally callow and callous toward the people in the pews weeping away. I suppose this happens to undertakers, too. I wonder if that experience prepared me better to accept the death of my loved ones. Coffins do not bring tears to my eyes, not the way I cry now when I remember little boys trying to grasp the meaning of death.

My other secret crying place was the big weeping willow back by the creek here at our home place. It had a big fork up among the branches where I could sit and view the land all around, completely hidden from mortal men. It seemed fitting to have a secret crying place in a weeping willow. The first time I cried there, I was watching my son running across the fields, calling to his dog. "Here, Dusty dog, here Dusty dog, here Dusty dog," he shouted, his voice rising and falling, so happy and free, the sound fading into the willow tree branches around me. With an awful rush, I realized that he would soon grow up. The boy would be gone. And the tears came. Later, many a day, I would sit there in the weeping willow weeping, and hear him still. It was as if the tree preserved his voice, as on an audiotape.

A few years ago, the old willow blew down. I was sad, of course. I had known that tree since childhood, even before I owned the property it grew on. But I was unprepared for what happened. We went back to look at the fallen tree with our teenage granddaughter,

Becca. When she saw it lying there prostrate, she started crying and ran off to be alone. I was totally caught off guard. She is much too young to learn about the need for secret crying places.

I had not realized that even though she did not grow up nearby like the grandsons, but only visited occasionally, she had a sentimental attachment to our place. Her mother had told her so many stories of playing under that tree. Later, when she was preparing to go off to college, she made a casual remark that she hoped her children would have a chance to learn about places like ours where sheep and children could run free, at least for awhile. Then of course I had to cry some more.

There is one memory I dare not recall unless I am in one of my secret crying places because I can never hold back the tears. Came a day I had to take a journey to a far-off hospital to see what was wrong with me. The family had all gathered around the dinner table and discussed my health where the grandchildren could hear, and, although we tried to make light of it, they were not fooled. We all said our goodbyes the night before my departure, still pretending there was nothing really wrong, and how I'd be back in a couple of days, and make sure the chickens got fed and watered while we were gone, tra-la-la-la-la. Next morning, Carol and I packed up the car for the three-hour ride to the Cleveland Clinic. Just as we were about to leave, from down the road we could hear the familiar sound of Evan's four-wheeler roaring along from his parents' home hardly two miles away. He had come to say goodbye one more time—for all he knew one last goodbye. As a teenager, dependent on his parents for everything, he had little in life to call his own, to stand apart as his own man. But he had his four-wheeler. He came all alone for one final farewell.

When we drove away, he followed us down the road. He followed us all the way to the highway, as far as he was allowed to go. He stayed with me to the very last possible moment. He had such a forlorn look on his face as I watched him through the rearview window that I could not stand it. But I dared not cry or

Carol would have melted. I set my jaw till it hurt. That memory, of a boy on his four-wheeler, framed in the rearview window, would always be in my mind, to bring tears to my eyes, but especially the next day when I was first introduced to the preposterous notion that I just might be dying. I had promised him one more basketball game in the barn.

CHAPTER 20

Facing Death

*A*t first, I figured it was just old age. Every day I had less energy, but the change was very gradual. Eventually, even walking to the barn I'd have to stop and rest a couple of times. The doctors found fluid around my right lung. At first they thought maybe I had pneumonia, but that didn't factor out. So they took a look at my heart and arteries. They were good for an old man who had gorged on butter and cream all of his life. That sounded like good news, but if my heart wasn't the problem, the other likely possibility was the dreaded word. Cancer. They checked my lungs. Okay there, too. Then they took a closer look into the pleural cavity around the right lung. No cancer showed up at first there, either, but looking back now, I can see that the doctors were thinking cancer still. A biopsy of the area around the lung followed. When I woke up from the procedure (no one says "operation" anymore) I was staring into Carol's face. Oh, those eyes. How often I had looked into that face, but always before it had been full of happiness. Now she had to tell me the bad news, and the sadness in her visage hurt me more than the realization that I had cancer. I could maybe deny my cancer but there was no way to deny that look on her face. The surgeon, looking rueful, was hopeful: "If you can think of yourself as lucky, this is a kind we can usually take care of."

And so began my battle with the big C, which sounds a bit grandiose since all I did was sit around while the doctors and nurses did all the battling. I will bore you with a few details because I wish I would have had something like this to read beforehand. The ordeal was not as bad as I thought it was going to be. The first thing was to get rid of the fluid around the lung. The surgeon put a pleural catheter in my side. The nurses taught us how to drain out the excess fluid every few days. We understood that this could go on for quite awhile. The surgeon mentioned, trying to be offhand, that he had a patient who had a catheter like this in him for two years. Oh. And then the patient got okay, right? Silence. I was not so stupid that I needed to ask. He died.

At first caretakers came to our house to make sure we were draining the catheter correctly. But Carol learned how to do it mostly on her own, reading all the directions. What I remember was how upbeat we both were about it. This would be over soon, we said, even though there was no evidence of that. And that is exactly what happened. The fluid starting drying up soon after the chemotherapy treatments began. In only a couple of months, the catheter could be taken out. That was done right in the office, no pain, no being put to sleep—a snap, really. I felt like a galley slave after having his shackles removed. I dared to think I was going to get well.

Before the chemotherapy, bone marrow samples were taken from the bone right above my butt to see if the cancer had gotten that far. Extracting the samples took only seconds and the pain of it was short, almost negligible. The results were negative. Radiation would not be necessary.

The chemotherapy treatments lasted six months, one day every month. I was getting off easy compared with many patients. Since

I thought I was dying, it is tempting to overdramatize the ordeal, but the truth is, the chemo was not all that bad. As I have said, fear was the worst part of it. The nurse said in the little speech she made at the beginning of the first treatment: "This is not going to be nearly as unpleasant as hearsay has led you to believe." And she was right. There was hardly any pain. There was fever and nausea the first night after a treatment, but not as bad as having the flu. I never had to take the pills the nurses sent home with me for nausea. Two Tylenols knocked down the fever. I did not lose any hair. I lost my appetite, and yet eating was necessary to keep up energy and limit weight loss. I never thought that eating would be something difficult to endure, but forcing down food was an ordeal. Giving up my evening drink of bourbon was, on the other hand, not at all a hardship. Even thinking about bourbon, I would almost vomit. So my weight went down, my cholesterol went down, and eventually so did the blood pressure. I joked that for people with problems in these areas, try chemo. The nausea would wear off by the third week after a treatment, so there would be about a week of near normality before the next treatment. As you can deduce, if the worst part of my chemotherapy was lack of appetite, it was certainly not the agony I had feared it would be. Even the total physical weakness that overcame me was not really hard to endure. When you are too weak to walk, sitting is a luxury. And I could still write while I was sitting.

A treatment would last about five hours. I liked having a private room for it. But later I didn't mind one of the big rooms, where as many as a dozen people might be undergoing treatments at the same time. At first I felt embarrassed to be exposed so to others, and they to me. But learning to talk with other patients, or just watching them, relieved some of the boredom of sitting there for hours. There was plenty of drama there to observe. Our mutual battle against cancer became a sort of rallying cry of camaraderie. But most of all, I was lucky to have a caring wife and daughter there with me. Both of them sat there through the long hours, as pert and positive as if we were waiting for news that I had won a Pulitzer or something. And the nurses were always solicitous and good-humored—very pleasant company. My way of hiding my fear was to try to joke about it all, and they were past masters at that art.

Fortunately, my daughter and her family lived in the Cleveland area, so I was able to schedule my treatments at the Cleveland Clinic, which is well known for its excellence. We could stay at Jenny's the night before and the night after if necessary. My doctors were all exceptionally kind and caring, and so were the nurses who assisted them. My main doctor was a specialist in the particular strain of the follicular lymphoma that was laying me low. When I talked about dying, he scolded me gently. He was sure he could put the cancer into remission. All the caretakers spent quality time with us, visiting and talking to me before each chemo session and going over my situation in detail. These meetings often had the air and spirit of impromptu parties, believe it or not. Once the doctors and nurses understood that we liked the humorous approach, they kept us laughing, and we sometimes kept them laughing. If I learned anything about the whole cancer event it is that humor is still the best medicine. It is infectious. If you show good humor, your doctors and nurses will return it, and that helps the healing process almost as much as the medicine.

Well, that's an overstatement, of course. What I was learning through my cancer was how much medical care was advancing in this day and age. One of the two fluids they were putting into my body contained what I'll call little bugs because I can never remember the right terms. They go scurrying around through the blood, hunting down and killing cancer cells like a pack of hounds chasing down a rabbit. I can't even imagine the monumental amount of research and expense that must have gone into this development and scores of other new ways to fight cancer. Cancer is not necessarily the kiss of death anymore. When I hear people deride socialized medicine, I can only shake my head in disbelief. No one, however rich, can afford to pay for what society is getting in medical help today. It takes all of us contributing, and even then I don't see how we are going to afford the degree of mortal immortality that I think will be possible in the future.

The Cleveland Clinic is a mighty big place, unnerving to someone like myself who lives mostly in solitude in the woods and shuns the public. When we drove up to the entrance of one of its buildings it was like pulling up to a grand hotel. We were fortunate to have daughter Jenny doing the driving. Nothing about the big city daunts her in the least. There were swarms of cars and people everywhere, along with all kinds of aides and valets to handle the traffic and help the sick people, provide wheelchairs if necessary, and give directions to the myriad offices and facilities. I felt like a mouse in a herd of elephants that knew I was underfoot and so were careful not to step on me. It was marvelous how well this system could handle the hundreds of people thronging in for medical care every day. The admissions people and receptionists, who check patients in, take their Medicare and insurance information and all that, were amazing. I was stunned because I had been ignorant enough to think that people in those kinds of positions were, well, you know, of average intelligence. But after I watched them process the constant line of patients to their proper treatment rooms or doctor offices, I knew that average minds would not last two hours in that job. About the fourth time I checked in at one desk (after being away a month, remember), I was standing there waiting my turn, feeling like a maggot in a swarm of maggots, and one of the receptionists looked up and sang out: "Hey, Mr. Logsdon, how you doin' today." Out of all the hundreds of people she handled every week, she remembered my name. "How in the world do you do that?" I asked. She just smiled and said some people are more memorable than others. But I checked her out and learned that this was her way to add excellence to a rather humdrum job. She evidently had a photographic memory and practiced little memory tricks to link faces and names. Her name was Micah. Here's to you, Micah, for putting a nice little shining light into my darker days.

Before a treatment, there was always "blood work" to do—I called it bloodletting. Nowadays, getting needles poked into one's veins to draw blood or to insert IVs has become routine. But the veins tend to give out over time where they are used repeatedly as ports of entry. Patients who need lots of IVs generally end up getting a catheter or port put into a big vein just under the chin through which the chemicals are administered. This is preferable to frequent needle-poking, but did not seem necessary in my case. Inserting IVs, however, became the most disconcerting part of the whole experience for me. Carol said it was because I am a big baby. But veins vary in the ease in which they accept needles, and some nurses are better at it than others. Some days, I would have to be poked a second or even third time, and the trick was to be very calm and forgiving when the nurse missed the first time. She was just as displeased as I was. If I stayed calm and jokey, she generally got it right the second time.

After the blood was drawn and sent off immediately to be diagnosed, and sometimes after X-rays or scans, we would meet with the doctors involved and their staffs. I learned to be prepared to do a lot of sitting around when waiting on busy doctors. I didn't really mind because when the doctors did show up, they took the time to talk a little while. That's why they were late. They were treating all their patients that way.

Jenny always had her laptop along, and we would go through my office emails, answer the ones that needed immediate attention, check my blogsite to read the latest responses to my posts. Being able to keep up with my work was a relief and made the time pass a little faster. I could also stay amused during these waiting periods by watching television. Normally I wouldn't find that interesting, but this was the time when the Republicans were trying to nominate a presidential candidate and they presented one of the most entertaining farces that I have ever seen on screen. To this day I thank them all for giving me something to laugh about through a difficult time.

After meeting with the doctor and his crew and learning the results of blood work and scans and X-rays, there would be more waiting out in the big open hall before the treatment. There were puzzles there, always in the process of being put together by waiting patients or their companions. Or of course there were magazines and newspapers to read. In one area musicians played their instruments. Marvelous. Almost everyone whiled away the time on smartphones, however. It occurred to me that in this day and age when museums are having a hard time luring visitors, they should put displays in big hospitals and in airports where waiting is part of the normal schedule. But then I remembered that one can call up museum displays on smartphones now. What a world we live in!

Finally, an always pleasant nurse would usher me into the treatment room. The nurses welcomed Carol and Jenny, too. This was a very important detail to me: Hospitals allowed a family member or two back into the place of treatment. It was so much easier for me to handle my fear with Carol and Jenny beside me. More important, wife and daughter always knew, with absolutely professional precision, the answers to questions I was asked. I depended on that. I tended to block out of my mind the vocabulary of medicine: the proper names for my condition, my pills, the chemicals they were giving me, and all that crap that I did not want to think about. I pretended that if I did not learn the language, I did not have to admit that I was sick.

The first step in a treatment, after I got propped up comfortably in a bed or stuffed chair, was a pill or a shot of Benadryl to make me sleepy, then two anti-nausea pills and two Tylenols. I was always offered water or fruit juice and encouraged to drink lots of both. Then the IV was inserted, and soon a nurse brought in the bag of fluid that she hung on sort of a hall tree with wheels on it beside my bed or chair. The fluid was ice-cold. The nurses checked and double-checked with one another and with me to make positively sure they had the right stuff. With so many patients undergoing treatment, they have to be supremely careful. I think over the last year I have given them my date of birth at least five thousand times.

The fluid dripped out of the bag, down a tube, and into my body. I could watch it drip. The arm into which it went got cold because the fluid was cold. Blankets were provided if desired. Usually by the time the treatment was underway the Benadryl had begun to take hold and I would grow sleepy and even gabbier than usual. Some patients are able to sleep through much of the treatment, which unfortunately was never my luck. I was too nervous to even read, although that is what most people do.

During my first treatment, the nurses hovered around me more attentively than they would later on, because there was no way to know how a particular patient was going to respond. I was hooked up to all sorts of monitors for blood pressure, oxygen content in the blood, and so forth. The nurses would keep asking me how I felt, and I, being the stupid male, was intent on pretending everything was fine and dandy even if it wasn't. During the first treatment, my arm started hurting and when I couldn't stand it anymore, they immediately went into action, stopped the infusion, shifted me around and adjusted things, scolding me for not letting them know every least bit of discomfort. Several times my blood pressure went worrisomely low and they made me lie flat on my back, which helped. I learned how to cheat on the oxygen reading. They would put a little thingamajig on my forefinger to measure oxygen content in my blood. It was supposed to be around ninety-seven, and if I really sucked in large amounts of air, trying to do so surreptitiously, I could raise it from, say, ninety-four to ninety-six, which passed muster. This was, well, whacko on my part, because the whole point is to have an accurate count. Besides, I wasn't fooling the nurses one bit. They have seen every deviant quirk the minds of old men can think up, and if you can get them talking, they make great stand-up comedians.

The hall tree on wheels, on which the paraphernalia of the treatment hung, was quite the amazing triumph of technology to an old farmer. It had its own batteries, so it could be unplugged and the dripping went right on dripping and the gadgets right on gadgeting for quite a long time using the battery for power. I could stand up, using the mobile hall tree as a sort of cane, hang all the tubes carefully on the framework, and go waltzing off to the bathroom. No problem.

The dripping sometimes stopped because of a bent hose or for various other reasons known only to the gods of technology. Then the thing started beeping, and of course I would start to panic. Maybe my body had stopped functioning properly and death was imminent. After awhile, I realized that, like all machines I have ever dealt with, this one was mysteriously contrary and was going to have a beeping fit every so often no matter what. A nurse would soon come in to make the proper adjustments. Sometimes the beep was just to tell her that one part of the infusion period was over and she needed to up the dripping speed. I had a little push-button gadget close to my hand that I could use to beckon a nurse if necessary. But after I had been through the process a few times, I no longer panicked at the beeping.

I must tell a story. Before the first surgery or procedure, when the docs were trying to figure out what was wrong with me, I was of course put completely asleep. But there was that drowsy stage right before sleep, during which the patient can get very talkative. Especially patients who are rather talkative anyway, like me. So before that first procedure, I felt compelled to tell the roomful of doctors, orderlies, and nurses that I had written a book titled *Holy Shit*, which at that time struck me as super-funny. I fell asleep soon after informing everyone of this important historical event. I forgot all about that little episode, of course. So in the operating room before the second procedure about a month later, I looked around at the gathered assemblage and tried to show that I was not afraid. In my most cavalier attempt at calm aplomb, I informed the group that there were some people there who looked familiar. Why I thought that would make me appear cool, I can't say. But one of the doctors, from across the room, spoke up for all to hear. "Yeah, you're that guy who wrote a book about shit." The whole room broke into laughter, and that's the last thing I remember until I woke up again.

There are all kinds of restaurants in and around the Cleveland Clinic, as well as stores and shops, so Carol and Jenny could get a break now and then while I sat there counting the drips of fluid. Sometimes, I could actually eat a little right during the treatment. For some crazy reason, I developed a bit of a yen for chocolate milk.

The tempo of the dripping fluid was increased about every half hour, so the second half of the bagful went out quicker than the first half. There is nothing slower than a dripping IV infusion. It is amazing how my mood could grow brighter just because there were four drops dripping per second rather than two. When the first bag emptied, a second of a different fluid got hung on the hall tree thingy and the same procedure was repeated. By this time, I understood the expression about "time standing still." But eventually a session would be over. No matter how weak I might feel, I could always walk out of the building and to the car. I would have crawled if necessary.

Sometimes, especially after the first two sessions, I felt well enough to enjoy Jenny's gourmet dinner when we got back to her house. (The lingering nauseous effect of a new treatment usually didn't start until the next day or so.) Again, I think of how lucky I was to be able to stay with family. I got to know my daughter and granddaughter better, for one thing. And Carol could take comfort in the companionship of family. She and Jenny and Becca had good long visits out of it all. I am fond of saying that for someone who does not believe in any of the traditional definitions of a kind and loving God looking down on us, I am some kind of proof that such a God just might exist after all.

Although my condition seemed to be improving and the cancer cells were diminishing inside me, I still had to deal with the grim reality that I was indeed facing death, as we all are, but now really, not hypothetically. I had already managed, long before cancer, to arrange my mind so that I did not fear being dead. After years of assiduous contemplation and after the experiences I relate here in earlier chapters, I had finally become convinced that the various religious beliefs about life after death were just plain ridiculous. I do not wish to criticize or belittle other people for such beliefs—I can see how they soothe many people facing death—but I had passed the mental point where that kind of solace made the least bit of sense to me. I had found another way to look at the process. Once I was dead, I was dead. Oblivion. I would not be in some weird place beyond place where I could see or be conscious of the world and all the people I loved in it and so worry about them. To be dead, to be oblivious to the mindfulness with which we embrace conscious life, was not a scary situation. That thought carried a sort of comforting solace. When I tried to explain that to people of faith, they would get a desperate little expression on their faces and start looking for a way out of my presence.

But making peace with the state of death was only half the battle. I had not yet made peace with the process of dying, of saying goodbye, of going through the agony of watching people watch me die. But the weakness, the nausea, the lack of appetite, the dwindling of sexual desire, a bit of loss in hearing and eyesight, and the never-ending round of doctor visits, was making the idea of dying not so fearsome as it appears to younger people. Nature has its ways of preparing humans for death, and I found myself understanding what my grandfather meant when he said that for those lucky enough to make it to their nineties, as he had, death was really relief. I also learned what he had meant all those times he had said to me that to remain reasonably happy about it all, it was good to take "just one day at a time." To do that did bring a certain resigned relief. For young people, the future is everything, but it is also fearsome in many ways because it is unknown. For the elderly there is just today. Maybe tomorrow will be another day, and so on, but by concentrating on the NOW, the only time that truly exists, there is a kind of contentedness. One learns to appreciate every little detail of the NOW, which is really the secret of happiness for all ages.

CHAPTER 21

One More Spring

*T*he cancer stayed in remission. Perhaps it was gone for good. Who could say? Spring was coming again, and I imagined myself reborn. I did not know how to think about myself. I had prepared my mind for death—if that is possible—and then had been granted a reprieve at least for one more spring, and maybe quite a few more. There was no big bang, OMG moment when I had learned about the cancer or after I found out that it was in remission. In both cases I just felt disembodied, as if my mind were hovering over me, watching my body the way a buzzard watches a sick sheep. I seemed almost like a foreign object to myself, a stranger in a strange land.

For the young, the future is real, inviting, intriguing, but rimmed with a tinge of fear, as I have said. For me, the old man, there was no future. Oddly, the emptiness and disinterest that a futureless life suggests was not as deadening as it might seem. Without concern for the future to distract me, I could face the present moment with unconditional concentration. The present was all I had.

A further advantage of this new perspective on life was a greater feeling of freedom over whether my contrary opinions about science or religion were going to irritate people and bring angry retaliation. I didn't have to be afraid of losing my job. I didn't have one anymore. I was not running for public office or trying to win a popularity contest. I was too old to care about human respect. Old men can be dangerous to society.

Not having much of a future, I also no longer cared to argue about issues, formerly my favorite pastime. Disputation, I now realized, thrived only in the unreal vocabulary of mental calculation, not in the raw, real world. I literally had no time for it. I began to abhor confrontation, which only destroyed tranquility and kept me from concentrating on the world outside my mind where the real unknowns waited to be discovered. I experienced a kind of intellectual liberation similar to the physical relief of not having to contend constantly with the distractions of sexual yearning that plague younger people.

In an unexpected way, advances in science and technology were also taking the onus out of my living without a future. One of my major interests in life was to show that political and economic freedom was not possible without food freedom and that forsaking food independence in favor of slaves and unsustainable machines to do the work was the basic reason societies declined and civilizations fell. The only way to prove or disprove that was to study past declines and falls more closely. We had before our eyes an earth that was literally strewn with the ruins of fallen civilizations, and electronic technology was now finding ways to make these ruins come alive again. Just recently explorers located the ruins of much larger and much more sophisticated cities in the jungles of Central and South America than they had hitherto expected, specifically in Honduras. Flying low over the impenetrable jungle, airplanes equipped with what was called lidar were finding and mapping these "new" ruins, doing in a few days what would take many years with land-based surveys. Lidar and other electronic methods suggested that something like an electronic time machine might be possible, allowing us to examine the past much more thoroughly than we could do so previously and applying that knowledge to the future. What if we could prove conclusively that because we take food for granted, those gigantic skyscrapers rising higher and higher over the urban landscape of our cities now will someday lie broken and shrouded in jungle growth, just like the ancient ruins? Such possibilities seemed exciting enough to keep me alive a few more years out of sheer contrariness.

Whatever science might do someday in the way of inventing a real time machine, I was determined to squeeze as much wonder and delight out of every passing moment that my energy could muster. When I did that, life became almost as dazzling and exciting as it had ever been. I still went through intervals when I cried too much, but it was kind of a sweet sorrow savoring precious memories. I kept singing lines from one of my very favorite songs, Noël Coward's "I'll See You Again," given new and deeper meaning by my situation: "I'll see you again/Whenever spring breaks through again."

In January, I was already thinking of enjoying spring again, the great reawakening time in nature. I stared out the window at the brown and seemingly dead stuff on the ground, or sometimes white and seemingly dead stuff. The one true fact of life was death, my mind would announce dolorously to me. But then it countered by pointing out that the only true fact of death was life. I replied, as if my mind were not quite part of me anymore, by humming "I'll see you again, whenever spring breaks through again," even though the last word of that song is *goodbye*. I intended to watch the earth renew itself in the minutest detail of which I was capable and rejoice in that renewal.

How soon into the winter solstice, indeed, did spring begin? I noticed little mounds of green moss in the woods already in January. Why had I not noticed them in previous years? Probably because I was too busy worrying about the future. A little research showed that these mosses actually start showing green in December. Nature never died completely, just slowed down in the cold time. Renewal was the constant, not death. Death was just the first step of renewal.

I fell to wondering what was going on down in the depths of the pasture pond in winter. I fashioned a dipper from a plastic jug and fastened it to a long pole so I could scoop water off the bottom of the pond through a hole in the ice. There were all sorts of almost microscopic bugs and plants in that water! Life had not stopped but only retreated a little. The fish, turtles, and frogs were down in the mud, more or less hibernating like humans would do if they had any sense. Humans were on top of the frozen water, beating each other with hockey sticks.

Behind the house, a bit sheltered from the cold, daffodils and snowdrops nosed above the ground in a January thaw, even with snow only a foot away. It seemed impossible. Surely they would be killed by cold weather yet to come.

The birds at the feeder outside the kitchen window gave no hint that this was the dead time except that the goldfinches wore their cold-weather brown business suits, not their sunny, summery yellow sport coats. Blue jays lorded it over the smaller birds, and I cheered when the red-bellied woodpecker would appear and put the bullies to flight. Not that it mattered much to the small birds. Nuthatches and downy woodpeckers darted in to grab seeds before the bullies could stop them. Cardinals were the only polite visitors to the feeder, demurely allowing even the little tree sparrows and chickadees to eat beside them. White-crowned sparrows showed up only when there was snow on the ground, and it bothered me that I did not know what they ate when the ground was bare. House finches were all too common but more welcome to me than the English sparrows that defecated on the deck railing much more than the other birds. Oddly enough, these sparrows, which generally live much more in the presence of humans than most other birds, were among the wariest. When I wanted to get rid of a flock of them, I had only to tap faintly on the window and they would whoosh away while other birds stayed put, trying to figure out where the tapping noise was coming from. Perhaps English sparrows have learned by their close association with us that we are nature's biggest danger.

It was good to see the tufted titmice back in residence. They went missing for a year, and we feared some change in nature's balance had taken them. Once more nature showed that it maintained balance by going from excess to shortage and back again. Not balance but teeter-totter.

Finally February came and with it a few more signs of renewal. The wild black raspberry canes had their own spectacular way of signaling awakening. In a warmish spell, when sunlight suddenly followed rain, the canes glistened in striking purplish hues. To my amazement the snowdrops did not die in the cold spells, and now when the temperature rose above fifty degrees Fahrenheit, their white blossoms, still tightly closed, appeared beside the vanishing snow. Close by, winter aconite stems, slightly doubled over, elbowed above ground. The daffodils stirred hardly at all, but their aboveground green tips were not killed, either.

In the woods, great horned owls began hooting their mating song in the evening. To me this was the first true sound of spring. Not to be outdone, the cardinals began singing in the morning as if it were already May. Could they feel the lengthening day under their feathers, or were they taking a cue from the owls?

As the snow melted, the pasture turned into a patchwork of white and brown, like an Andrew Wyeth painting. Thaw time. The thaw sang mutely of spring as clearly as the owls did with muffled hoots. But then the snow came again. I curled up beside the woodstove, thinking about how, in so-called death, the warmth was the wood's way of celebrating the years of sunlight stored in its fibers. Life burned brightly, even during blizzards.

The weather warmed soon enough, however, and despite the snow, the sap was rising, promising more wood to stay warm by.

Now was the ideal time to tap maples. Rising sap said more about the coming of spring than the calendar did, and dwellers of the woods knew that the first sap, before the air warmed enough to swell the maple buds, made the best syrup. The yellow-bellied sapsuckers were the first to the table. I no longer had the energy to tap trees, but I knew how to look pathetic in front of friends and family who did, and they gave us syrup. There was nothing as tasty as syrup only a few days from the tree. I once conjured up a theory about how sap straight from the tree just might be a good spring tonic, full of pure and undefiled minerals from deep within the earth. If I drank enough of it, perhaps I would still be able to steal second base at age ninety. I drank quite a lot of it one day and the subsequent diarrhea allowed me to run to the bathroom almost as fast as I could run to second base. Was this perhaps the derivation of a common derogatory term in our area, *sappy*? I had once more transgressed the ancient wisdom: "All things in moderation." Thinking about that, I wondered if humans might be genetically modified to take all things in moderation. Maybe Monsanto Claus was on to something really good after all.

Even though at the beginning of March there was little sign of the great awakening, I could feel spring in the air. When I walked down the lane to get the mail, the sun felt noticeably warmer than it had in December, even though the thermometer registered about the same temps. Also, walking on the lawn, there was give to the sod, a certain softness that told me the frost was out of the ground. Was it that warmth that was allowing me to walk, now, all the way to the mailbox and back to the house without tiring?

To see the woods lose all the white snow patches and turn completely earthy brown was relief in itself. I kept watching for the first tinges of green. I spied tiny blades of bluegrass in protected sunny places by the barn. The chickens spied them, too, and gobbled away. I hobbled away, to the pasture. On the south side of the woods, the sheep were also finding new bluegrass. It reminded me of how wrong it was for grazing experts to belittle bluegrass as a profitable pasture crop just because, in dry August, it went dormant. Here it was providing food when the other grasses and clovers were still asleep. And I did not have to plant it. Bluegrass came to us free from nature.

At breakfast one morning, Carol spied a strange bird in the woods. She gasped audibly and grabbed the binoculars. Sure enough, a pileated woodpecker was pounding away on a big dead limb of a shagbark hickory tree. It tore off strips of bark to get to the rotten wood underneath and, looking for bugs to eat, tossed it out in chunks as big as Ping-Pong balls. We had seen this spectacular creature, big as a crow, only once before in our grove.

A few mornings later, we spotted a pair of sharp-shinned hawks skimming along just above the treetops. We knew from other years that they would soon be building a nest. But we had already been tipped off that they were back from the south. The crows had been clamoring loudly the day before. Crows believe it is their duty to harass hawks. If you want to stage an effective protest rally, hire crows. In this case, they had concluded through the winter that they owned the grove, and these newcomers were shattering their sense of security. Oddly, the returning buzzards, soaring higher in the sky, brought no response at all from the noisy demonstrators.

The hawks must have been especially hungry because one of them tried to catch a squirrel right out where we could watch the ludicrous show. The squirrel showed no fear when one of the hawks, perched on a fallen branch nearby, suddenly made a sort of halfhearted lunge at it. The latter nonchalantly hopped away maybe ten feet and then just sat there in utter disdain, chattering what I am sure were choice squirrel cuss words. The two repeated this little maneuver several times, always with the same result. Maybe the hawk was practicing for when the new little squirrels that it could handle would emerge from their nest holes. Maybe it was just having fun.

March brought with it one of my favorite jobs, burning brush piles that had been collecting from cutting firewood over the past year or so. I used to think that it was good to keep piles of brush around for wildlife protection. But that's a good way to guarantee that your garden will be ravaged by rabbits, groundhogs, raccoons, and opossums, all of which love the safety of brush piles. Now that much of the wildlife around us was on a population binge, it didn't need protection. And brush piles, themselves, have a way of overpopulating, too.

I picked days that were windless for brush burning so no sparks or flaming leaves could blow away and start a fire where I didn't want one. But a wee bit of breeze was nice to drive the flames into the pile. The ground around the piles was sodden, so I didn't have to worry about the fire getting away from me. I set the brush ablaze with wads of newspaper and then sat down on an upended five-gallon bucket to watch and dream. I kept a trusty pitchfork nearby to push outer branches nearer into the flame if necessary, and then, as the flames consumed the pile, to pitch unburned ends of branches at the exterior of the fire into the hot coals. I can't explain why this job was so peaceful to me except that it kept me comfortably warm without much physical activity. The fire did the work. As the branches burned, they sometimes sang as the moisture boiled out of them. The cats slipped up beside me and stared at the flames, too, waiting for a mouse to run from the burning pile. A rabbit bounced out, hopefully an evening meal for the owls, hawks, or coyotes. Even the sheep came around, sniffing, reminding me that they needed a fresh bale of hay. Eventually the hens sifted through the woods, scratching up leaves as they came, finding bits of something to eat even this early in the year. They responded to the singing flames by singing joyously themselves. Then a rustle of wings came suddenly into the trees in the nearby grove and a chorus of croakings and cluckings and wheezes and whistles told me that the red-winged blackbirds were back from the South. They marked the real first day of spring better than the vernal equinox. They reminded me of one of those tone-deaf choirs, each singer rapturously chorusing away, blissfully unaware that his or her notes did not harmonize very well with the notes of the others. But because of the joyous unity of the flock, the concert sounded almost as harmonious as the Robert Shaw Chorale.

The barn disappeared in April. It always did. The trees in the grove between it and the house leafed out, slowly at first and then faster as the month ended, and the barn would not be seen again until fall. Now came the grand awakening for sure. We got out the hoes, the mowers, the tillers, the seed. We needed to be ready so that the instant the soil was dry enough or the grass tall enough, we could get something done before the neighbors did. This was American culture in action. Though at the beginning of the month the fields and gardens were soaked, water lying everywhere, past experience told us that somehow in the second half of the month there would come a time, a "window of opportunity" as the commercial farmers put it, when the soil might be dry and warm enough to plant early corn. I didn't really have to watch for the window of opportunity but just listen from an easy chair. In our neighborhood, the very minute the soil was ready to work the big tractors would begin to rumble throughout the land, as much a part of the song of spring as the owls were in February. I was amazed at the discipline of the farmers. With so many acres to plant, they desperately needed to start as soon as possible, but they never sprang from the starting gates until the ground was absolutely ready. They knew if they tried to cultivate our clay soils too soon, only a havoc of hard clods and poor germination resulted. It took me years to achieve the proper discipline to calm my eagerness, even in the garden. Now in old age, without the volatile energy of youth, you would think it would be easier to wait, especially since I knew that May-planted corn invariably did better anyway. Seed corn salespeople pushed April corn planting because then the farmers might have to buy more seed and plant over.

But I could not help myself. Maybe this would be my last season, and I wanted to exit the scene with the earliest corn in the neighborhood. The potato ground from last year, with excellent tilth from plenty of rotted manure and compost, was almost dry enough, by April 23, at least on the tops of the humped ridges where the potatoes had grown the year before. Maybe I could gamble and, for the first time in neighborhood history, have corn up before my siblings did down the road. I was able to hoe and rake up a fairly nice seedbed all right, stopping every few minutes to rest in a chair. What the heck. Spring was here and everything was going my way.

To ruin what little chance the seed had for germination, three nights of near-freezing temperature followed the planting. The kernels never stirred in the cold dirt. Well, two of them did. I waited ten days for more corn to peek above the ground. Nothing. I dug up some of the seeds. They had only barely swollen before they rotted.

By now everyone in the neighborhood had corn planted. I put out two more rows. I was using old seed to save money, which had always worked for me before. One of my sisters intimated that I was an idiot. So I got worried and planted yet two more rows with newly purchased seed. But I left the old seed of the second planting just to see. Sure enough, both plantings came up very nicely because now of course the soil was warm enough to sprout the seed. If I had just waited until the commercial farmers had started planting, my corn would be two inches tall like theirs instead of just coming up. The folk saying of the future will be: "Plant corn forevermore, when the monster tractors roar."

But by the end of the month, everything—in the garden, in the pasture, in the woods, in the orchard—was a lush convergence of showers, new growth, and feverish activity. Carol hurried from one job to another. I limped after her, dragging my chair. Between rains, we got the early peas in, some potatoes, onion sets, and radishes, with lettuce in the cold frame. I was full of joy, still able to live like I loved to live. And I was still learning. The plots we planted to potatoes and peas had been covered heavily the summer before with aged barn manure and leaves, and this mulch had mostly rotted away into a nice layer of compost and humus. Instead of horsing the tiller over the ground, which I barely had the strength to do, I just gently hoed and raked over that top layer and planted—so much easier than getting out the tiller. I wondered if postmodern technology would return to well-crafted hand tools and away from costly, complicated machines.

The spring peepers peeped, their music signaling the arrival of birdsong choruses. Folklore said that the peeping was a prediction of rain next day. Another myth. Frogs peep because they like to. A spring peeper got into the house once when we carried a big potted plant into the basement. It liked music, and when classical music came on the radio, especially Beethoven, it responded with its own chorus of song, no matter the weather outside. In our part of the Midwest, rain falls or threatens to fall about every three days, so in the clumsy logic of human abstraction, any noise could be interpreted as a forecast of rain. The tiny frogs sang intermittently almost every day now and of course, being spring, rain fell about every other day or so, too. I made it a point to listen to the frogs closely. They were talking to one another and did not give a peep whether it rained or not. One of them would start singing in the roof gutter above the deck where I sat. Another, in the oak tree nearby, would answer it. A third would take up the discussion from a hickory tree on the woodland edge, and then the whole grove would burst into cheering as lustily as fans at a major-league ball game. The real wonder was that so much noise could come from such tiny creatures.

Soon after the peepers started singing, the toads pushed up through the woodland soil where they had spent the winter and journeyed to the pond in the pasture where they had begun life. The books say they come back every year to their birth ponds. They had memory. Their minds were not as dull as humans assumed simply because they did not write books or run for public office. That something so ugly could sing so beautifully was another wonder. I started making daily trips to the pond that only recently, under ice and snow, had seemed so dead. The toads, when not singing, gave themselves over to an orgy of sex, two, three, or four clinging to one another in what I assumed was toad ecstasy. Was it ecstasy that produced the music, too, not so unlike human song following ecstasy?

The red maples bloomed. The red-winged blackbirds were right there, cheering the trees on. Not so long after that we heard the song sparrow. No music from human vocal cords could equal it to my ears. Then the first round of wildflowers seemed to ooze out of the ground. The snowdrops bloomed, whiter than the snow that so recently had covered them. Winter aconites followed, turning drab lawn into patches of sunny yellow. The dandelion flowers were still at early bud stage, when they make good salad with the new leaves. I looked now for morel mushrooms. I thought that with all the dead ash trees in the woods, killed by the emerald ash borer, I would find plenty of these tasty fungi growing under them. No such luck. The old-timers said the roots needed to rot another year to bring on the mushrooms. Again I was reminded about how the decay of one kind of life meant not death, but the renewal of another kind.

As the weather warmed, blooms on daffodils, grape hyacinths, bluebells, hepatica, and Dutchman's-britches magically appeared. We had put out small plantings in earlier years, and now they were increasing and multiplying without any help from us other than not mowing until they had matured. I read a magazine article that complained that daffodils were becoming invasive on farms! Other varieties that we had not planted, like rue anemone and wild geraniums, appeared all on their own. I thought we had lost the anemones for awhile, only to find this year another little patch of them beside the lane in the woods. In earlier years, their cousin woodland anemone came into the woods all on its own, too, but then disappeared. The comings and goings of wildflowers mystified me. Botanists said that their seeds could lie in the earth for years and, when conditions were right, they would germinate and grow. How else could one explain the white violets—Canada violets, the books call them—that suddenly started growing in the yard and spread all over? Had they marched all the way from Canada? Or ridden here on the wings of fairies? The philosophical, if not botanical, lesson seemed so apparent. The earth was not a burial ground, but just a waiting room where all life gathered strength to move up again.

One of the thrills this year was seeing the honeybees again after all the bad news in the media about their demise. When you get old and have no future, you spot paranoia so much more easily than in earlier years. The bees had endured another winter in a wild hive, which Carol found later, without assistance from humans, even though they were plagued by disease and chemical pollution as much as humans were. I felt close to them. Maybe they had their own kinds of cancer to deal with. They were buzzing all over the blossoms on the very first day the winter aconites started blooming. Earlier, when I chain-sawed a tree that had fallen over the path to the barn one warm day, they were all over the place, licking sap-soaked sawdust.

Because of the late spring, April had hardly reached its full glory before the greater glories of May were upon us. May was for me the highlight month of the year— rhubarb custard pie in the first week, strawberries and cream in the last. May's first calling card came from the lilies of the valley as their fragrance wafted into the house from the patch right outside the dining room window. Likewise, my nose knew when May was about over when the wild grapes bloomed—a perfume more delicately delightful to me than any other in nature. In between came a rapture of flowers so bountiful I could hardly contain myself. All the many years of planting some of them, and providing the right habitat for others, brought on what I might consider a grand finale for my enjoyment, except that I knew next year the whole glorious show would be back again, with or without me.

The great white trilliums outdid themselves, and in so doing taught me another lesson. This wildflower was on the endangered species list in some places, and I wanted our grove to be one place where they were always protected. The white blooms were quite large, more like a domestic flower than a wild one. Getting them started in virgin woodland soil was not difficult, only slow. For ten years the three plants I set out, in three different locations, showed little inclination to increase and multiply. Then, just as they did start to spread, the deer found them. (Oddly, the deer did not bother the toadshade, also a trillium, growing nearby.) I saved one of the nicest plants by covering it with a five-gallon bucket at night. Carol sprayed a couple other plants with something that was supposed to keep the deer away. Maybe it did, but the unsprayed plantings, which I had given up to fate, prospered, too. Lots of little seedling trilliums started showing up around the three original plantings. This spring many of them bloomed. The parent plants that the deer had decapitated the previous year blossomed as well, half a dozen blooms per plant. Again, the resilience of nature confounded me. For reasons I can't explain, the deer did not bother them so much this spring, and in each of the three locations there were at least ten plants blooming. Moreover, the patches were spreading, with scores of little seedling trilliums popping up all over. This rare endangered species was spreading like Canada thistle!

I knew from other areas that deer in large numbers could despoil a woodland of all of its wildflowers. Here we had obviously not reached that state of overpopulation. Some three to five deer traipsed past our gardens and house regularly. They nibbled on almost everything, including fruit tree leaves, and even on the cursed multiflora rose, Canada thistle, and sour dock, as if to make up for their larceny of our "good" foliage. They seemed to want to taste everything, even tomato leaves, but not much of any one thing, except maybe the hostas. They used to nibble the native columbines excessively, but now this wildflower was spreading all over, too.

It was the rapidity with which the flowers spread that was so amazing. In the first years, they did not move much at all. But after that there were new plants everywhere. The Jacob's ladder had spread from a couple of plants to a patch twenty feet in radius. The planting of waterleaf had gone viral, and I feared it might become a pesky weed. But it was so pretty. I had about given up on getting bloodroot started because both plantings I made years ago died out. Then, this year, under the big white oak in the lawn, three of these precious flowers bloomed. I was fortunate to notice them at all because bloodroots usually bloom for only for a day or two, and without the blossoms I would not have noticed the leaves. Where had they come from? I do not remember planting any there. The woods fairies did it, I say. Science might be nice but magic would suffice.

We were not able to mow much lawn until May, and so the grass around the house was a carpet of golden dandelions and purple violets. It was so beautiful that we did not want to mow. Greenswards of clipped grass are beautiful, too, no doubt about it, and quite necessary in many instances. If we would quit mowing altogether, seedling trees would spring up and grow to four feet tall in two years. We knew that from experience. We sometimes got the feeling that nature was a green monster ready to swallow us up if we let it.

But like all things good in the human world, we have carried our love for manicured grass to extremes. There are more acres in lawns in the United States than in commercial food crops, and in fact lawns are the largest irrigated "crop" of all. On something over forty million acres of turf, we spend thirty billion dollars a year. Homeowners use ten times more pesticides per acre of lawn than farmers do per acre of crops. In fact, one of the most audacious examples of hypocrisy is the suburban homeowner who piously criticizes farmers for polluting our waterways. We burn eight hundred million gallons of gas mowing lawns, and statisticians say that we spill seventeen million gallons every year just refilling our lawn machines. If so, that beats the *Exxon Valdez* spill of ten million gallons. The pity of all this expenditure is that the grass, which mostly gets thrown away, could be producing who knows how much milk, meat, eggs, and manure fertilizer for a growing world population, a large portion of which is half starving to death.

Lawns, say their defenders, provide a neighborhood with more air-conditioning than air conditioners do. They certainly soak up more rain than driveways and parking lots. Lawns provide lots of other good things, too, but now there are new reports out that say soil temperatures under lawns are higher on average than farmed soils. This warmer soil increases CO_2 emissions into the atmosphere more than cornfields do. Oh, what a low-down attack on our most sacred of all Sacred Cows. Our lawns might be causing climate change.

The phoebes nested on top of one of the barn beams again. The nest was so situated that the cats couldn't get to it. How had the birds figured that out? I could stand under the nest, barely three feet out of my reach, and the mother bird would not budge unless I made a sudden movement or noise. She had figured out that I wasn't going to harm her, either.

Bluebirds sat on the deck railing near the bird feeder or the oak limb close by, not for sunflower seeds, which they never ate as far as I could observe, but with their eyes peeled on the lawn below. Suddenly they would drop to the ground, grab a bug, and fly off to a hole in a nearby dying hickory tree that they had turned into a nest. There had been nuthatches and starlings interested in that hole, too, and through binoculars we watched them settle the real estate problem. Why the bluebirds won the argument I couldn't figure out for sure, but I think they borrowed a trick from the wrens who took over the hollow gourd we always hung beneath the deck. The wrens filled the cavity so full of twigs that only they could wiggle down underneath, where their eggs were located. I was fairly sure that's what the bluebirds did in the hickory tree. The nuthatches did the same with another tree hole in a black oak nearby that starlings always tried unsuccessfully to take over.

Now in May the birds returning from the south overwhelmed us. First there were the hummingbirds. How do these tiny creatures navigate thousand-mile trips to return to us and then know they need to fly daintily against the window to remind us that it is time to hang out the feeder of sugar water? Those tiny little bird brains knew things. They had memory, too, like the toads. Every spring they talked to us this way. And they quit tapping when we got the feeder hung. I had to wonder. So-called non-rational animals could outfly us, outrun us, smell more keenly, see more sharply, and hear the slightest sounds from much farther away. When I closed the door of the house on my way to the barn, nearly a football field away, the sheep heard the door closing and immediately started baaing. Since all knowledge supposedly comes through the senses first, was it possible that non-humans had a refinement of knowledge, of retrieved information, of experience, that "rational" humans couldn't even imagine, let alone achieve?

Next came the Baltimore or northern oriole, which liked to eat oranges of all things; then the scarlet tanager, which we always saw sitting on lower branches of big trees in the woods, never anyplace else; and then the brown thrasher arrived, trying to outdo the mockingbird in mimicry but always failing. Then the tops of the trees around us started humming and buzzing with migratory warblers we could not see without binoculars. The warblers mostly were not well-named because they were poor singers, but their colors were so stunning and varied that I couldn't believe that I had lived half my life, mostly close to nature, before I learned that our woods in May were full of flying jewels.

So overwhelming was the beauty and life of May, smothering my senses in warm breezes, in birdsong, in flower fragrance, and in sunlit dazzle of every color in the spectrum, that I wanted to wrap my arms around it all, hold it to my body, and scream "Stop!" I wanted May to last forever. But now I understood that it was only because nature changed every month, every day, every moment, that it could come again. Only through change is permanence achieved. Be still, frantic human. To understand immortality, embrace mortality. I stood a long time staring at a fallen daffodil.

What was left of it was splayed out flat on the ground, the leaves turning from green to ivory to brown, the flower stems mostly golden in the sunlight. Here was the plant that so cheered me through March with its refusal to give in to frost, then in April laughing at the retreating cold with a burst of budding flowers. Even now, crestfallen, it had a certain beauty to it, spread out there on the ground so piteously. But it was only me doing the pity thing. The daffodil was not dying but only on its annual way down into the ground, so that it could come to decorate April another year.

Every year there came the perfect day for me, sometimes in late May, more often in early June. This year it was June 4. There were strict criteria that had to be met to qualify for perfect-day status. June 4 was warm, but not too warm, sunny but only sunny after a nice shower the day before had thoroughly moistened the earth. The garden and the field crops were growing lushly. We had caught up on weeding. The iris patch was in full bloom. No mosquitoes, deerflies, or sweat bees were swarming about yet. There was no faraway place I had to travel. The lawns were mowed and no rip-roaring motor shattered my ears. But I had to wait until evening for the all-important detail that was necessary for the title of perfect day. The evening came, perfectly still, no wind, with the sun sifting sideways through the trees in the grove. Then came that final touch of perfection: the lucent song of the wood thrush ringing crystal-clear and clean through the lower limbs of the trees.

In June I watched for indigo buntings. Like so much of the natural world, these small, dark bluish birds could be very close around the house and we might not notice them. I only realized they summered here when they nested in the pole beans, literally right under our noses. This June, while I rested in my chair near the beans when they were just beginning to climb their poles, here came an indigo bunting, flitting from one pole to another, as if checking them out. Did it know that the vines would eventually grow up to make a great place to hide a nest later on? Or was this just happenstance?

Through June, the pace of nature's growth slowed ever so little but noticeably. The great awakening was drawing to a close. I watched the antics of the flycatcher in the bur oak next to the deck. It sat on a limb all through long, shady afternoons, darting out occasionally to snatch bugs. Perhaps it got bored because once it darted out and grabbed a falling leaf. Another time it captured a rather large insect, settled back on its limb and let it go, then chased it again.

The catalpa trees bloomed so thickly with their whitish flowers as to almost hide their strange broad leaves. Then the blooms fell, covering the ground like snow. I tried not to look. I didn't want to be reminded of snow. The dainty little blue-eyed grass in the pasture came and went so fast I could easily have missed it if I weren't watching. I consider it the last of the spring wildflowers, although one could argue that. There is no last or first in nature, just a continuum. Time is the property of the abstract human mind.

The strawberries finally quit producing. We thought we were growing the old Senator Dunlap variety after newer varieties did not seem as tasty. But when we tried to buy more Senator Dunlap plants, they turned out to be something different from our first purchase, so we were not sure of the identity but only that the earlier-purchased variety was much better. So I kept it going all these years. Varieties did not "run out" as was often claimed. To keep strawberries productive, whatever the variety, one must be sure to start a new patch every year or every other year with year-old rooted runners, and not let the patch get overcrowded with old plants.

The crowning glory of our taste buds in June were peas and new potatoes. No billionaire, however rich, or no exotic restaurant, however expensive, could provide vegetables any tastier than these two, simply boiled a little and served side by side. We planted both on the same day in late April, and they were ready to eat by mid-June. The potatoes of course were only small yet, about the size of Ping-Pong balls. We robbed them from the plants that were the first to bloom by pushing our hands under the thick leaf mulch and groping into the humusy soil until our fingers found the little potatoes. We took only a couple from several hills so that most of them would grow to goodly size by regular harvest time. Gold in them thar hills.

The peas were more tedious to harvest because of the shelling. Many people grew the kinds that are eaten pod and pea together, but we vastly prefer shell peas despite the work involved. It is very important to harvest the peas at their tenderest stage, when they do not fill the pod to the point where it feels hard and solid to the touch. Shelling peas reminds me of my mother. She would gather us children around like a hen with her chicks, in the shade of a tree where a June breeze kept the sweat out of our eyes, and we would shell contentedly while she told stories about the fascinating days before automobiles. She claimed that she and her brother, as children, got into big trouble for throwing rotten watermelons out on the road from the cornfield where they were hidden, trying to scare passing horses and buggy riders. I tried to keep grandchildren busy shelling by offering a dollar for every pod they found that had eleven or more peas in it. We grew Green Arrow, which could occasionally sport such long pods.

In June, fittingly at the end of spring, I sold my sheep. I had to—just didn't have the vigor to take care of them properly any longer. I penned them in the barn the night before to be ready for the hauler and next morning fed them the best bale of hay I had left. All the years of shepherding reeled off like a film in my memory as I climbed into the haymow. How many times had I pushed hay down into their mangers and then stood in the comforting darkness and listened to them grunting contentedly as they munched. There were also all those wonderful memories of children and lambs bouncing across the pasture accompanied by a grown man who had been lucky enough to find paradise on earth. I loved it all so much it had never dawned on me until right now that it really *really* had to come to an end. To climb up into the haymow and throw down hay one last time was too much for me, but this was my secret crying place, so I just let the tears fall. Other shepherds not far away were buying the sheep, so I did not have to watch them go off to the stockyards and maybe could visit them occasionally. For two days, I mired myself in self-pity and wondered if maybe all the stuff I was writing about non-death was just bullshit. But the sweet memories that hurt so much soon began to heal me. The tears stopped. Memories were the compost of the thinking process, enriching the mind world, never dying as long as there were people who kept on remembering and the written word stayed safe in books or in the electronic cloud-god in the sky.

The summer solstice came, the end of the great awakening. I still heard the sound of sheep baaing plaintively for me to turn them into a fresh pasture plot. I still heard me calling them as they came rushing, phantom-like, to the gate. In fact I could still hear, as clearly as if it were yesterday, cousin Adrian calling his sheep over these same hills three-quarters of a century ago. As long as there was memory, even sheep were immortal.

But there was no time for looking back sadly, as the glories of midsummer were upon us, like roasting ears five minutes from the garden and Kentucky Wonder pole beans cooked slowly with ham hocks. And then the golden days of autumn would arrive and life would begin its descent into the earth so that spring could come again. Winter would hardly be upon us when the first signs of next year's great awakening would appear. Death was only a mirage of the human mind. And so I faced the future that did not exist and sang my favorite song. In the deepest sense of the words, I'll see you again—we will all see each other again—whenever spring breaks through again.

Acknowledgments

----------◆----------

*M*y thanks to publisher Margo Baldwin at Chelsea Green and all the people there who work so hard to make my writing more presentable, especially Ben Watson, Brianne Goodspeed, Bill Bokermann, Melissa Jacobson, Laura Jorstad, and Helen Walden.

My gratitude also goes to the doctors and nurses who have kept me healthy enough the past two years to keep on writing, particularly Doctors Byron Morales, Robert Dean, Peter Mazzone, Sudish Murthy, Kriti Mittal, and Joseph Cacchione, plus so many wonderful nurses, especially Amy, Kandi, and Susan.

Two of the chapters in this book—"Killdeer Woman" and "Georgie the Cat"—originally appeared in slightly different form in the 1977 anthology *Listen to the Land: A Farm Journal Treasury*. My thanks to all those people at *Farm Journal*, now long passed away, who started me on my writing career and always generously allowed me to use early writings in later books and magazines.

Needless to say, I would be but a speck in the sands of time without the love and dedication of my dear life partner, Carol, daughter Jenny and her husband, Joe, son Jerry and his wife, Jill, and three grandchildren for whom this book is especially written: Evan Logsdon, Alex Logsdon, and Rebecca Cartellone.

ABOUT THE AUTHOR

A prolific nonfiction writer, novelist, and journalist, Gene Logsdon has published more than two dozen books, both practical and philosophical. His nonfiction works include *A Sanctuary of Trees*, *Holy Shit*, *Small-Scale Grain Raising*, *Living at Nature's Pace*, and *The Contrary Farmer*. His most recent novel is *Pope Mary and the Church of Almighty Good Food*. He writes a popular blog, *The Contrary Farmer*, as well as an award-winning column for the Carey, Ohio, *Progressor Times*, and is a regular contributor to *Farming Magazine* and *The Draft Horse Journal*. He lives and farms near Upper Sandusky, Ohio.

the politics and practice of sustainable living

CHELSEA GREEN PUBLISHING

Chelsea Green Publishing sees books as tools for effecting cultural change and seeks to empower citizens to participate in reclaiming our global commons and become its impassioned stewards. If you enjoyed reading *Gene Everlasting*, please consider these other great books related to gardening and agriculture, permaculture, and nature and the environment.

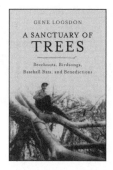

A SANCTUARY OF TREES
Beechnuts, Birdsongs, Baseball Bats, and Benedictions
GENE LOGSDON
9781603584012
Paperback • $19.95

HOLY SHIT
Managing Manure to Save Mankind
GENE LOGSDON
9781603582513
Paperback • $17.50

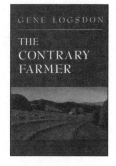

THE CONTRARY FARMER
GENE LOGSDON
9780930031749
Paperback • $19.95

SMALL-SCALE GRAIN RAISING, SECOND EDITION
*An Organic Guide to Growing,
Processing, and Using Nutritious Whole Grains
for Home Gardeners and Local Farmers*
GENE LOGSDON
9781603580779
Paperback • $29.95

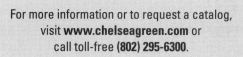

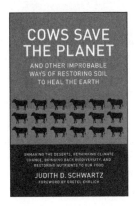

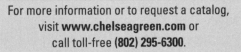